The City of Westlake Village
and the Westlake Village Foundation
are pleased to make possible this limited edition of

The City of Westlake Village

A HISTORY

"A City in the Country"

History is the witness that testifies to the passing of time,
it illumines reality, visualizes memory, provides guidance in daily life,
and brings us tidings of antiquity.
—Marcus Tullius Cicero, 106–43 B.C.

THE
DONNING COMPANY
PUBLISHERS

The City of Westlake Village

A HISTORY

by James B. Henderson

Dedication

With sincerest appreciation, this book is dedicated
to my wife Lucille, my greatest supporter
and my inspiration for over sixty years.

J. B. H.

Steve Mull, General Manager
Barbara Bolton, Project Director
Joni Walters, Project Researcher
Barbara B. Buchanan, Office Manager
Richard A. Horwege, Senior Editor
Jeremy Gray, Graphic Designer
Scott Rule, Director of Marketing
Travis Gallup, Marketing Coordinator

Library of Congress Cataloging-in-Publication Data

Henderson, James B. (James Beattie), 1915–
    The city of Westlake Village—A history / by James B. Henderson.
        p. cm.
    Includes bibliographical references and index.
    ISBN 1-57864-197-7 (alk. paper)
    1. Westlake Village (Calif.)–History. 2. Westlake Village (Calif.)–
History–Pictorial works. I. Title.

F869.W49 H46 2002
979.4'92–dc21

                                                    2002035115

Printed in the United States of America

CONTENTS

ACKNOWLEDGEMENTS

I wish first to recognize those who assisted in the development of this work:

Winfred G. Allen, Ph.D.–Editor

Jeff Friedman–Consultant

Audrey J. Brown–Assistant City Manager

Mark Rutherford–Councilman

Much appreciation is owed to a large group of people who consented to interviews on their recollections–and in some cases, records–about the development of Westlake Village. A number of these contributors were involved in the decision-making process from the initiation of the project–particularly John L. Notter, the president of American-Hawaiian Steamship Company when the concept of Westlake Village was first developed.

Clint Airey
Justice Herbert L. Ashby
Victor Austin
Berniece Bennett
Rev. Robert C. Bos
Joseph Bowman
Grant Brimhall
Ray C. Brownfield
Kris Carraway-Bowman
Amy Commans
James E. Emmons
Jack Fish
Roger Garretson
Rabbi Alan Greenbaum
Mary Lou Gold
Donald Goodrow
Margaret Hansen

Rodney Hansen
Fred Howse
Richard Hus
Russell Huse
Jim D. Johnson
Pastor Robert B. Lawson
Marie Marewa
John H. McDonough
Patricia Russell Miller
Robert Morrison
John L. Notter
Harold Poett
Joyce Prouty
Ray Prouty
Doris Rufener
Raymond B. Taylor
Tony Tramonto

Donald Zimring, Ph.D.

Much of this history is based on newspaper articles collected and filed by Joyce and Ray Prouty–from *The Acorn*, the *Thousand Oaks Star*, the *Las Virgenes Enterprise*, the *Daily News*, the *News-Chronicle*, and the *Los Angeles Times*.

Additional and valuable written records were provided by our Daniel K. Ludwig Library, including a biography of its namesake.

6

Section I

Community Timeline

THE EARLY YEARS

The first existing records for this area tell about the 1769 expedition of Captain Gaspar de Portolo and his band of sixty Spanish soldiers, who left Velicata in Baja California in search of an inland route to Monterey Bay. Accompanying the group was Father Juan Crespi, who served as both spiritual advisor and scribe for the venture. After traveling through the San Fernando and Santa Clara River Valleys they turned toward the coast. Although familiar with Monterey Bay from the sea, they did not recognize it from the landside, and continued as far north as San Francisco Bay.

On the return trek, their food supplies ran low and the men became ill and discouraged. They survived by eating one of their pack animals each day, until friendly Indians alleviated their suffering by providing them with fish and other food.

On January 13, 1770, local natives guided them into Potrero Valley, and on the next day they stayed near another native village. Father Crespi's diary describes the location as "a plain of considerable extent and much beauty, forested in all parts by live oaks, with much pasturage and water." So on January 14, 1770, the desirability of Westlake Village was first recognized! Father Crespi named the area *El Triunfo del Dulcisimo Nombre de Jesus* ("The Triumph of the Sweet Name of Jesus"), and some parts of that name still exist in Triunfo Canyon Road and Triunfo Creek, and Father Crespi's name is memorialized on a high school in the San Fernando Valley.

In those early days, ships supplying the northerly settlements often took three months to sail from San Blas in Mexico to Monterey because of the very strong headwinds. It became essential to find a land route over which large groups and essential food and supplies could travel. In 1774, Captain Juan Batista de Anza, commander of a presidio in Arizona, headed a large expedition to establish a satisfactory land passage over which those settlements could be supplied. He traveled de Portolo's route through this area and in late February made camp in the area that was to become Westlake Village. With a second and even larger group, de Anza passed this way again in 1776, and his scribe notes, "some watering places like those of El Triunfo and Los Conejos"—the very first recognition of the area's rabbits! As many more groups passed through this region in ensuing years, the route became known as El Camino Real.

By 1800 a grant had been requested for the approximately fifty thousand acres that was to become Rancho El Conejo. The property extended from what is now the eastern boundary of the City of Westlake Village to the Conejo grade. In 1803, California Governor Jose Joaquin de Arrillaga granted an undivided interest in the land to two former soldiers, Jose Polanco and Jose Ignacio Rodriguez. Polanco may have farmed in the area prior to the grant, but by 1804 he had moved to the presidio of Los Angeles. After the Mexican revolution against Spain in 1822, Alta California became part of Mexico. That same year the commandant of the Santa Barbara presidio, Captain Jose Antonio Julian de la Guerra y Noriega, petitioned then Governor Pablo Vicente de Sola for an undivided half of Rancho El Conejo. In view of Polanco's abandonment of his claim, and de la Guerra's services, the governor granted the eastern portion of the Rancho (then known as *El Triunfo*) to de la Guerra—in the name of the Emperor of Mexico.

After the U.S.-Mexican War of 1845–1847, the Treaty of Guadalupe Hidalgo ceded Alta California to the United States. It also pledged the United States to honor legitimate land titles. California became the thirty-first state on September 16, 1850, and in 1870 Ventura County was formed from the southern part of Santa Barbara County. It was not until 1872 that the U.S. Surveyor General finally confirmed the 48,672-acre ownership of Rancho El Conejo to the de la Guerra interests and the Rodriguez brothers' heirs. One week after that confirmation, Howard W. Mills and John Edwards bought the undivided 24,000-acre de la Guerra half for $55,000—about $2.30 per acre! Records show that Mills built a small home at approximately the location of the Westlake Bay condominiums and started a settlement in what is now the Westlake Village part of Thousand

Howard Mills.
(Courtesy Stage Coach Inn Museum)

Oaks. In 1876 the first school in the area was started in Mills' house.

In 1881 Howard Mills suffered financial difficulties and left the area. The San Francisco Savings Union foreclosed his then six-thousand-acre ranch. A young Canadian, Andrew Durkee Russell, heard about the very desirable property and took a stagecoach from Santa Barbara to inspect it. On the coach, a very talkative land speculator told Russell about a ranch he was going to buy, and Russell realized it was the same land. When the coach stopped in Ventura, Russell rented the fastest horse available and rode to the ranch site where he met Jake Gries, the ranch manager. After a wild buckboard ride around the ranch, Russell gave Gries a twenty-dollar gold piece to seal the deal—just as the stagecoach arrived with the speculator!

On October 31, 1881, the brothers Andrew Durkee Russell and Hannibal M. Russell signed a trust deed in Santa Barbara County for 5,968 acres in the eastern part of Rancho El Conejo for $15,000—$2.50 per acre! For the next eighty years the Russell family added to their land holdings, and continued to successfully operate the ranch, which they called *Triunfo*, from Father Crespi's original name for the area in 1770. The history of those years is well documented in books written by Russell family members. (See Bibliography)

In 1926, the newspaper magnate, William Randolph Hearst, bought most of Triunfo Ranch, on the speculation that oil could be found on the property. (It wasn't!) The Russell family retained 165 acres where the houses were located and leased back the rest of the property from Hearst. They continued to raise cattle, but no longer farmed any grain crops, which they had found not as profitable. In 1943, a successful automobile

Andrew Russell. (Courtesy Stage Coach Inn Museum)

dealer from Los Angeles, Frederick S. Albertson, bought the main property from Hearst, and one hundred acres from the Russell family. Albertson then operated the ranch and continued to raise cattle. He imported a number of Texas Longhorns, which he rented out to motion picture companies; the cattle could often be seen looking over the fence at passers-by on Decker Road (later Westlake Boulevard). When Albertson put the ranch up for sale in 1962, the American-Hawaiian Steamship Company tendered a bid of $32 million, but one John Gottlieb protested the sale, claiming that he had a prior verbal commitment to buy the property for $30 million. However, his claim was not upheld and working with Truesdale Construction Company as a consultant, American-Hawaiian closed the deal in 1963 with a short-term loan of $30 million from Chase-Manhattan Bank.

In 1966, a long-term loan was arranged with Prudential Insurance Company that in turn was converted to an equity interest in 1969 with American-Hawaiian retaining all management and development functions. The partnership was ultimately dissolved in 1973 with Prudential receiving 9,000 acres of the property, including the 4,700-acre North Ranch site, plus 723 apartment units.

THE PLANNING

In 1964, American-Hawaiian commissioned Bechtel Corporation to perform a comprehensive planning study for the entire 11,780 acres of the Albertson Ranch. While the ultimate development varies somewhat from the final Bechtel report, the basic elements for what were to become the reality of the "City in the Country" were all established in that plan.

That study included not only the existing geology, hydrology, natural features, and land uses—the clear canvas of the open ranch upon which the long-range concepts would be portrayed—but in two years of effort by literally hundreds of specialists, all elements of a successful community were studied. Housing types, circulation, land use standards, utilities, health care, churches, cemetery, recreational facilities, public safety, neighborhood identities, commercial and industrial developments, venture development costs, interim investments and schedules, construction costs, and sales projections were all evaluated in detail prior to breaking ground for this new, master-planned community.

As noted elsewhere, some features of the community—such as the lake—were not included in the Bechtel studies. And others, such as high-rise residential towers at the western end of the lake, were never built! However, this careful and detailed

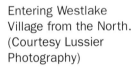

Entering Westlake Village from the North. (Courtesy Lussier Photography)

First Neighborhood.

Westpark.

Watergate. (Courtesy Lussier Photography)

Southridge Trails.

Lakeshore. (Courtesy
Lussier Photography)

14

The Trails. (Courtesy
Lussier Photography)

Westlake Colony.

planning laid the groundwork for what was to become a model for other community developments both in this country and abroad. Among the groups who came to study this new and comprehensive approach to community development were those from Asia and Europe.

Probably the most extensively planned community in the world up to that time, Westlake Village was designed to meet the following eight objectives as detailed in the Bechtel report:

To take full advantage of the position of Albertson Ranch in the Los Angeles region.

To provide a spectrum of land uses and community facilities in proper balance to serve all the residents.

To preserve and enhance the natural beauty of the site.

To satisfy a wide variety of housing needs.

To foster community identity and civic pride.

To establish comprehensive standards for location and space for all public and private facilities.

To provide a circulation system for the efficient transportation of people and goods.

To encourage contemporary designs of sites and buildings.

This laid the groundwork for the vision that Daniel K. Ludwig had for "A City in the Country."

Westlake Village founder Daniel K. Ludwig with then governor Ronald Reagan.

15

As the development progressed, D. K. Ludwig hosted numerous groups, which came from the East Coast, Asia, and Europe to observe and study the project, taking back with them concepts, which they then employed in their own planning.

Summer Shore. (Courtesy Lussier Photography)

Oak Forest Estates.

Westlake Island.

Three Springs. (Courtesy
Lussier Photography)

Parkwood Estates.

17

Westlake Renaissance.

Southshore.

Each developer and contractor operating in Westlake Village was required to adhere to the goals and standards of the original planning, and to maintain the ambience of this master-planned community. All homeowners were, and still are, bound by Covenants, Conditions, and Restrictions (C.C.& R.s) included with their property deeds. With few minor exceptions, the numerous homeowner associations have enforced those rules. The result after more than thirty years is excellent maintenance and landscaping throughout the residential areas.

18

Westlake Pointe. (Courtesy Lussier Photography)

Below Left: First Neighborhood—Freedom Square with commemorative Camino Real bell. (Courtesy Lussier Photography)

A key concern, then as now, was the preservation of the indigenous valley oaks (*Quercus lobata*). When a large oak tree had to be removed from the grounds of White Oak Elementary School, then under construction, a trench was dug around it and the root ball was encased in a wooden box about twelve-feet square. It was then permitted to stabilize for a time.

In December of 1971 it was transported by truck-crane to its new home at the Westlake Village Inn, placed in a prepared location and guy-wired—where it exists today, healthy and strong—and at a cost of only $13,000!

Below: Oak tree transplanted in 1971 to Westlake Inn—still healthy in 2002! (Courtesy Lussier Photography)

As early as 1969, it became evident that a local government would be better able than Los Angeles County to provide needed local services. The Las Virgenes Chamber of Commerce authorized a study to determine the viability of founding a new city with essentially the same area as the Las Virgenes Unified School District—about fifty square miles. Helen Funkhouser, a former Connecticut state assemblywoman, was appointed chairperson of a small group, which included Captain Fred Howse, then senior captain of the Cornell Road Fire Station, and James B. Henderson of Westlake Village. After about ten months of studies and meetings it became evident that potential income for such a new city would fall far short of even minimum needs.

The subject remained alive and the first of three groups based primarily in the Agoura area met in 1972 to again review the subject, but based on a smaller area. Henderson also participated in that short-lived effort.

By the early 1970s the need for autonomy had become even more evident. The City of Thousand Oaks had a bill introduced in Sacramento by their assemblyman, Kenneth McDonald of Ojai, which would have permitted them to annex the north side of Agoura Road in Westlake Village, plus the commercial lakefront properties. A small group of First Neighborhood residents, headed by James Henderson, became concerned and started to plan their opposition, especially after a luncheon meeting at the old Californian Restaurant in Calabasas with Thousand Oaks Mayor Richard Hus and City Manager Glen Kendall. Kendall frankly acknowledged their interest was in converting the Westlake Village Golf Course (then zoned highway-commercial) into all commercial, sales-tax-producing uses. After many telephone calls, newspaper coverage of the opposition, one television news story, and a visit to Sacramento for a meeting with the chairman of the subcommittee that was studying the proposed legislation, the bill was "pigeon-holed" and eventually dropped.

In the late 1970s, a second study group was formed in Agoura with Berniece Bennett and Jim Henderson of Westlake Village participating. That group, chaired by attorney Stephen Saroian of Agoura, reviewed a number of scenarios, one of which included the area from Woodland Hills to Thousand Oaks. Westlake Village was included in some of the plans but not others in which only the commercial sales tax-producing areas were to be encompassed. It became evident that taxes from a master-planned community like Westlake Village—with all its infrastructure in place—would have to be used primarily for the betterment of the Agoura area. Then another group headed by Ernest Dynda of Agoura split off from the Saroian contingent on June 9, 1980, and started their own cityhood investigation. They were quite open about their desires to include only the commercial and industrial areas of Westlake Village in their proposed city with the knowledge that such action could—under the codes then in effect—require the residential portion of Westlake Village to eventually become part of their city without a vote of its residents.

In early spring 1980, a meeting was held at the First Neighborhood Community Center to hear a presentation by a member of the Saroian group, who exhorted the audience to become part of their Agoura effort. When he warned that the commercially zoned Westlake Village Golf Course could become "an airstrip, or even an ammunition dump" unless the area joined with Agoura, the seeds of "going it on our own" were sowed. After the Agoura split, it became even more evident that a study should be made to determine if incorporation of Westlake Village (Los Angeles County) was a viable alternative.

On March 11, 1980, a dinner meeting was held to discuss the procedures for incorporation, and the information required to determine if such a move would be economically and politically feasible. In attendance at the Velvet Turtle Restaurant were Ruth Benell of the Los Angles County Local Agency Formation Commission (LAFCO), Grant Brimhall, city manager of Thousand Oaks, Berniece Bennett, Ray Brownfield, John McDonough, and James Henderson of Westlake Village, plus Justice Herbert Ashby of the Appellate Court.

At the meeting Ms. Benell noted that a common practice of "negative" incorporation was about to become state law. That practice had been used in over one hundred cases and allowed incorporated cities to take over unincorporated areas with at least twelve registered voters—without a vote of the areas residents! With that information, the group realized that expeditious action was imperative.

On March 24, 1980, another meeting was held at the Bennett residence and the decision was reached to establish a committee whose purpose would be to study the practicability of incorporation—financially, physically, environmentally, and politically. It was agreed that the group would be identified as the "Cityhood Study Committee."

The next meeting was held at John McDonough's home on May 8, 1980, to further lay out plans for work to be accomplished and sources to be consulted. The Cityhood Study Committee met again on June 11, 1980, to assign duties as follows:

Chairman: Berniece Bennett

Vice Chairman: Financial Studies and Report: John McDonough

Recording Secretary: Peg Hansen

Legal Counsel: Justice Herbert L. Ashby

Environmental Studies and Report: Ray C. Brownfield

Publicity and Correspondence: Rodney Hansen

Treasurer and Petition Collection: James B. Henderson

After statements in the press on July 17 that cityhood leaders in Westlake Village were "going on their own," the Dynda group in Agoura announced on July 22 that they were abandoning all claims to Westlake Village industrial and commercial areas.

A July 25 press release announced to the public the make-up of the new Committee and its purpose—to compile facts and figures for study before deciding on any specific recommendations.

On September 4, 1980, the Committee held its first "open" meeting at the First Neighborhood Community Center to obtain the views and ideas of

Cityhood Study Committee. Top row: Rodney Hansen, Margaret Hansen, James Henderson, and Herbert Ashby. Bottom row: Ray Brownfield, Berniece Bennett, and John McDonough.

residents. The very considerable interest of community members was evidenced by the questions asked and the support voiced at the meeting.

As the Committee's efforts progressed, Ruth Benell, the director of LAFCO, provided much guidance and help. When the studies showed that a new city would not only be economically feasible, but would likely have a $170,000 surplus the first year, the Committee discussed details of the proposal with twelve of the homeowner association boards in the area. A positive reaction was received from all boards.

The Committee mounted a drive to obtain the 825 signatures in favor of cityhood, representing 25 percent of registered voters, as required by the county. By September 12, 1,233 signatures had been obtained—almost 35 percent of the voters—and the drive was then called off because the county was charging the Committee fifteen cents to verify each signature!

After more than nine months of intensive effort, the Committee presented the application for cityhood to LAFCO on December 20, 1980, along with seventy-five copies of the Environmental Impact Report, many copies of maps of the proposed 5.4-square-mile city with 3,557 registered voters, descriptions of the areas involved, 1,233 voter signatures, and a $500 filing fee. LAFCO scheduled a public hearing on the application for March 11, 1981, at which time the application was approved unanimously and referred to the Board of Supervisors for their review and consideration.

On May 14, 1981, the Los Angeles County Board of Supervisors held a hearing on the application. After reviewing LAFCO's affirmative recommendation and a statement by Berniece Bennett, the Board unanimously approved the application. At that time they also set the date of November 3, 1981, for balloting on cityhood and the election of five at-large City Council members. Supervisor Kenneth Hahn spoke about the history of city formations, noting that Westlake Village was the eighty-second city to be incorporated in the county, and that from start to finish the effort had taken only thirteen months! The entire Board hearing was concluded in 14 minutes!

The seven Committee members then retired to the county cafeteria and toasted their victory with cups of coffee.

The Campaign

Cityhood Study Committee members preparing cityhood application. Left to right: Ray Brownfield, Jim Henderson, Berniece Bennett, Rod Hansen, and John McDonough. (Courtesy *News Chronicle*, December 12, 1980)

Once the county had approved the concept of cityhood for the Los Angeles County side of Westlake Village and had set the date for the election on both cityhood issue and the selection of five Council members, the work of the Cityhood Study Committee was essentially complete.

By mid-summer 1981, sufficient interest had developed that sixteen residents from a number of different neighborhoods (two of whom had served on the Cityhood Study Committee) had filed their candidacy papers for the five Council seats:

Berniece Bennett, First Neighborhood
Robert Benton, First Neighborhood
Kerry Caramanis, Southshore
James Cowen,* Parkwood Estates
Margaret Durse, Southshore
Katherine Diederichs,* Westlake Trails
Crosby E. Fentress, Southshore
William H. James, First Neighborhood
Bonnie Klove, Oak Forest Mobile Estates
Archie Latto, WestPark Apartments
Saul Nadel, Westlake Island
John H. McDonough, Westlake Trails
Franklin Pelletier, The Ridge
Lionel Salin, Westlake Trails
Irwin Shane, Oak Forest Mobile Estates
Mary Suski, Westlake Trails

* Withdrew

Considerable electioneering took place over the next few months with signs, mailing fliers, and door-to-door visits by many of the candidates. There was also activity by those few opposed to the concept of cityhood—primarily letters to newspapers questioning the need: ("another layer of government," "increased taxes," "poorer services," etc.).

CHRONICLE, Thousand Oaks, Calif., Sunday, December 28, 1980

A debate was also held between Sheldon Greenberg for the opposition and Kathleen Gordon for approval.

Another issue arose less than a week before the election—opposition to the new city using the name *Westlake Village!* Even though permission had been received from Prudential for the use, and the Post Office supervisor had advised that both sides of the county line would continue to use that address, serious concerns were expressed. At a meeting of the Joint Board of Homeowner Associations on October 28, 1981, representatives of five associations in Ventura County insisted that the new city-to-be should select another name because, according to a press report, "the Ventura County side of the community would lose its identity as part of Westlake Village and property values would decline if the area become known as Thousand Oaks (which, technically it is)." (*News-Chronicle* October 29, 1981) There was even an implied threat that one opposed homeowner was ready to initiate legal action to prevent use of the name. Berniece Bennett, a candidate and former chair of the Cityhood Study Committee, closed the discussion stating that, regardless, the name would be *City of Westlake Village*. A candidates' forum was held on the evening of October 30, 1981, at the First Neighborhood Community Center—a procedure that has been followed in every City Council election since that time. Thirteen of the sixteen candidates presented an opening statement to an audience of over one hundred residents. Each in turn then answered audience questions posed to them by the moderator from the League of Women Voters. The candidates then gave closing statements. Archie Latto and Franklin Pelletier spoke in favor of rent control for the (then) WestPark Apartments and the Oak Forest Mobile Home Park. John McDonough and Berniece Bennett explained how the studies conducted earlier for LAFCO demonstrated that a new city would be economically viable and would guarantee controls to help preserve the Westlake Village quality of life, as well as insure orderly growth and provide for increased police protection. On that same date, the *Thousand Oaks News-Chronicle* endorsed the concept of cityhood for the Los Angeles County portion of Westlake Village.

ELECTION DAY

Top: Fire Station 144. (Courtesy Lussier Photography)

Tuesday, November 3, 1981, saw a 51 percent turnout of Westlake Village voters versus 11.2 percent countywide! Eighty-one percent voted for incorporation—1,553 in favor and 366 against, thus positioning Westlake Village to become Los Angeles County's eighty-second city after the ballot certification scheduled for November 23.

The sixteen candidates, all of whom during the campaign had spoken in favor of cityhood, had also pledged to maintain, and wherever possible improve, the enviable lifestyle that exemplified Westlake Village. When the final tally was in, the five winners and their vote counts were:

John H. McDonough	1,303
Berniece Bennett	1,229
Franklin Pelletier	1,081
Irwin Shane	634
Bonnie Klove	545

An unsuccessful candidate filed one challenge against Mrs. Klove's election, because two of her supporters, when checking the voter roles at the Fire Station were seen to be wearing Klove T-shirts. The challenger then paid the county to run a recount of all the ballots cast at fifteen cents per ballot, and found his count reduced! Another candidate also filed a challenge for the same reason but later requested that it be withdrawn.

On Thursday, November 24, the Los Angeles County Board of Supervisors officially declared the results of the election, approved a package of agreements for conversion of authorities from the county to the new City of Westlake Village, and set the date of Friday, December 11, 1981, for the official incorporation of the new city.

Right: First City Council. Left to right: Irwin Shane, Franklin Pelletier, Mayor John McDonough, Bonnie Klove, and Mayor Pro Tem Berniece Bennett.

The newly elected City Council members, none of whom had any experience at starting or running a city, faced a prodigious task with only a few weeks to make it all come together. Once again, Ruth Benell of LAFCO provided valuable guidance and input. Just a few of the questions that had to be answered were:

When and where do we hire a city manager? A city attorney?

How large an office will be needed and where?

Do we need any other employees and what kind?

How much money will we need and from where?

How do we set up a budget for our new city?

When will the bills start coming in (police service, etc.)?

When will we get funds, what bank will we use?

In a series of unofficial meetings, the successful candidates addressed these and other questions, aware that the city should be ready to function in just a few weeks. The California Contract Cities Association recommended three people as candidates for interim city manager. After interviews, the team decided on Fred Bien, highly experienced as an interim city manager for new cities He agreed to take on the job for a few months, and proved to be of invaluable assistance.

SETTING UP A CITY

Operating as teams of two, the Council members-elect hired Velma Quinn as acting city clerk and Patricia Myers as deputy city clerk and executive secretary; rented six hundred square feet of office space for the staff at $540 a month; opened a bank account with funds provided initially by some Council members-elect (the new city's first real income was from sales taxes received in January 1980); bought office equipment and furniture; hired Patrick Coughlin of Richards, Watson and Gershon as city attorney; and interviewed several police departments before deciding on the Los Angeles County Sheriff's Department. Additionally, at Ruth Benell's suggestion, Berniece Bennett and John McDonough visited the City of La Habra Heights to learn all possible from a city of about the same size as Westlake Village. On that visit they met City Manager James E. Emmons who was later to become the city manager of Westlake Village.

Additional duties included studies of several options for library operation and for planning—in both cases the decision was reached to contract with the Los Angeles County operations as most familiar with area needs.

Friday, December 11, 1981, Westlake Village finally, and officially, became a city. It was a day of celebration, starting with an 8:30 a.m. breakfast for all the new City Council members in the offices of County Supervisor Mike Antonovich, followed by a 9:30 a.m. press conference to introduce the new City Council members to the media. At 4:30 p.m. that day, the official incorporation documents were recorded at the County Board of Supervisors' office, at which time the new city became a legal reality!

Official incorporation document.

At 7:30 p.m. on that evening, the new Council held its first meeting at the First Neighborhood Community Center before an audience of well over two hundred residents and guests, where the oath of office was administered to the five new Council members by Justice Herbert L. Ashby of the Fifth District Appellate Court (former member of the Cityhood Study Committee). Father Thomas O'Connell of St. Jude's gave the invocation, followed by some historical background presented by Joseph Bowman (formerly with Prudential Insurance Company), who gave a brief presentation on the founding of Westlake Village in 1966 under the direction of Daniel K. Ludwig. Colors were presented by Boy Scout Troop 775 and the flag salute followed. Supervisor Antonovich advised that at 4:30 p.m. this day Westlake Village had officially become Los Angeles County's eighty-second city, and that the "Certificate of Completion of the Incorporation of the City of Westlake Village" had been recorded. He then presented the new city with a plaque memorializing the event.

In brief ceremonies, the new Council then elected John McDonough as the city's first mayor, and Berniece Bennett as the first mayor pro tem—

which according to state law, were to be the highest and second highest vote-getters in the election. All the new Council members then offered brief comments, after which Berniece Bennett presented Plaques of Commendation to the members of the Cityhood Study Committee (Ashby, Brownfield, the Hansens, Henderson, and McDonough). Many presentations were made to the new city, among them by Ventura County, the City of Thousand Oaks, the cities of Lancaster, South El Monte, Artesia, and the California Contract Cities Association. Kris Carraway, representing the Westlake Community Hospital, presented bouquets of red roses to the two ladies on the new Council, along with a congratulatory plaque for the city.

The newly hired acting city manager, deputy city clerk, and the city attorney were introduced to the community, gave brief comments on what their duties would be in the daily operations of the city, and were sworn in. Their positions were then officially confirmed by the passage of the city's first three Resolutions. Fifteen more Resolutions were then passed, covering subjects as diverse as employment agreements and agreements to utilize Los Angeles County services for health services, animal control, and ambulance service. Then the new Council passed the city's Ordinance No. 1—providing

for Los Angeles County ordinances to remain in effect and declaring the urgency thereof. Five more ordinances were also passed, including a moratorium on certain development projects—a subject of concern during the election campaign.

And so the new City of Westlake Village was finally a reality—up and running just one year, eight and one-half months after the first meeting of the Cityhood Study Committee—a new record for any city incorporation in Los Angeles County!

Mayor McDonough adjourned the first City Council meeting at 8:55 p.m. and invited the large audience of city residents and the many guests to join in a cake and champagne social hour, hosted by the Westlake Village Junior Women's Club.

On Tuesday, December 16, the Council received welcome news that the County Board of Supervisors had voted to allocate $131,200 to the city for street maintenance and repair—but only for the period up to June 29, 1982—the end of the county's fiscal year.

The Council met again on Wednesday, December 17, and made the decision to employ James E. Emmons as the city's full-time city manager at $30,000 a year, with the understanding that he would continue to serve his present employer, the City of La Habra Heights, until April 30. It was noted that Emmons had started his city manager position there at age twenty-four—as the youngest city manager in California.

In further business that night, Interim City Manager Fred Bien was asked to investigate the costs and state requirements for installation of traffic lights at the Lindero Canyon and Triunfo Canyon Roads intersection, adjacent to the Oak Forest Mobile Home Estates. He was also requested to look into possible stop signs at two other Lindero Canyon Road intersections—at Foxfield Drive and Thousand Oaks Boulevard. Thirteen more Resolutions were passed covering a wide variety of subjects including employment agreements and assignment of tax assessing and collection to the appropriate Los Angeles County agencies.

The Council also directed the acting city manager to start negotiations with a local bank for interim financing up to $10,000.

One final meeting was held in 1981—on Tuesday, December 23. At that session, committee and other appointments were made:

Shane and *Pelletier*—Rent Control
    Committee
Bennett and *McDonough*—Golf Course
    Preservation Committee
Pelletier and *McDonough*—General Plan
    Committee
McDonough and *Bennett*—Police Service
    Committee

Klove and *McDonough*—Lake
    Management Representatives
Klove and *Shane*—Street Lighting, Street
    Maintenance Committee
Klove—Investigation of Mobile Home
    Park conversion to ownership

Representatives to several organizations were also chosen:

Westlake Village Joint Board—
    Berniece Bennett
Westlake Village Chamber of Commerce—
    Irwin Shane
League of California Cities—
    John McDonough
California Contract Cities Association—
    Franklin Pelletier
Southern California Association of
Governments—
    Berniece Bennett

The Council also voted for the new city to stay in the Los Angeles County Lighting District. An engineer from that agency advised the Council there were 823 streetlights in the city, and the estimated costs for electricity and maintenance for the upcoming Fiscal Year '82-'83 was approximately $144,200.

The meeting closed on a high note with notification that the city's income from sales taxes in fiscal '82-'83 would be about $100,000 higher than previously estimated, due to an increase in the city's registered voters.

The seminal year 1982 was a period of intensive learning for the new Council members, and their time was almost totally committed to the effort. Each meeting seemed to bring new challenges and new questions. Rent control for the mobile home park and WestPark Apartments, the need for a General Plan, renting of permanent space for a City Hall, financial issues, hiring the needed staff, contracting for police protection and engineering services, adopting an Environmental Impact Report, and dealing with city resident's concerns were just some of the issues that had to be resolved—and some of them demanded early action.

Among the high points in 1982 was the hiring of James E. Emmons as the city's permanent city manager—still the youngest city manager in the state! Michael Jenkins succeeded Patrick Coughlin as city attorney, and Ray Wood joined the team as the city's treasurer—a position he performed with distinction until his retirement in December 2000. Rick Vena became the city's first planning director on a part-time basis shared with his county job.

Among the matters that demanded Council time was the spate of cat killings that started to become a problem in March. In retrospect, the issue now seems almost ludicrous, but at the time demanded so much attention that the Council passed an urgency ordinance. First Neighborhood posted a $1,500

The First Full Year

reward, and people patrolled the green-belts at night—all to apprehend the "cat killer" identified by county animal and psychology experts as a young man with some surgical skills. At the end of summer, using ten cat carcasses sent by the Sheriff's Department, an expert at Pomona College identified all the cats as victims of coyote attacks!

Certain other high points were noted. In June the Council passed the new city's first full year ('82–'83) budget at $1.9 million!

Ribbon cutting at first City Hall. Left to right: Lisa McIlquam (Miss Westlake Village), John McDonough, Bonnie Klove, Cathie Wright, Irwin Shane, Ed Jones, Bobbi Feidler, Berniece Bennett, and Franklin Pelletier.

31

Some stressful issues had also arisen during the year and extension of City Council members terms in office was one of them! Between changes in state laws and Los Angeles County rulings on allowable election dates for cities, the Council members were faced with the choice of either shortening the terms for which they had been elected, or lengthening them by nine months! There was reluctance on the part of some on the Council to vote themselves longer terms, but many people in the community noted their satisfaction with the Council's operation of the new city and convinced them to extend their terms; the vote was taken accordingly on November 12.

In October, residents of Westlake Canyon Oaks were threatened by the Simi Wildfire, which spread from that area as far south as Thousand Oaks Boulevard. Fire equipment from both

Los Angeles and Ventura Counties responded quickly as many homeowners wet down their roofs with hoses to prevent flying embers from igniting them. As a result of that occurrence, the Council in November adopted an ordinance requiring all new homes to have fire-resistant roofs.

Another occurrence in October caused considerable concern in some regions, but little inconvenience here— our 213 area code was changed to 818.

A controversial issue arose toward the end of the year: should the Council vote themselves a salary to help with the expenses incurred by the members in performance of their duties? After considerable public discussion, the Council deferred action on that item until the new year.

On the occasion of the city's first anniversary in November, outgoing Mayor John McDonough observed that our incorporation was "not a vehicle of change, but a means of preserving what we have." This is a concept still true twenty years later!

When, in November, Berniece Bennett succeeded John McDonough as mayor, the Council looked back on 1982 as a year of accomplishment, intensive education on the details of local governance, a few frustrating experiences, but with a feeling of assurance that the new city was going in the direction the voters intended.

32

John McDonough hands over the gavel to the new Mayor Berniece Bennett, November 1982.

State law requires new cities to develop a General Plan within thirty-six months of incorporation. The new Council decided to start the process almost immediately. A bid package was prepared early in 1982 and submitted to a number of contractors specializing in such work. In realization that much local input would be required to supplement and guide the preparation of such a plan, the Council appointed a twenty-eight member Citizen's Advisory Committee to work with the selected contractor. The charter of that Committee was to provide to the contractor input and guidance on the local community, its needs and desires. (Appendix C)

At that time the state required that nine elements were to be reviewed in the preparation of a General Plan:

Conservation	Seismic Safety
Open Space	Public Safety
Land Use	Noise
Traffic Flow	Scenic Highways
Housing	

These elements were mandates to control and to act as guides for future growth. Because of the legal requirements of state law, the greatest emphasis was on the Housing Element.

After an in-depth review of five proposals received in response to the bid requests and interviews with several of

the bidders, the Council entered into negotiations with Envicom, Inc. In April 1982, a contract was signed with Envicom at a not-to-exceed price of $82,000 for performance over a period not to exceed ten months, and with a guarantee that the final report would meet all state requirements. The price was divided into two elements: Study and Preparation of Documents at $74,250 and Meetings with Council and Citizen's Advisory Committee at $7,680. The city's first General Plan was completed on schedule and was filed for future guidance as development went forward in the new city.

With good reason, the control of development was a particularly sensitive issue with the Council. The Los Angeles County Board of Supervisors, knew that the November 3, 1981 vote for cityhood had been successful and would relegate all land-use

City of Westlake Village General Plan

Prepared by: ENVICOM CORPORATION • Economics Research Associates • Greer & Company

decisions to the new city after the official date of December 11, 1981. Nevertheless they approved the Three Springs development for 481 homes—just nineteen days before the Council could take over that control!

Shortly after the city was founded, the new Council passed a four-month moratorium on all grading and building. In March 1982 the Council extended that freeze for eight more months and by emergency ordinance in November of that year extended it another year. Aware that some projects had been started before the cityhood election, the Council requested the Citizen's Advisory Committee to study and to make recommendations on such projects. Based on the Committee's report and concern for some developer's prior investments, the Council approved most projects on a case-by-case basis.

One project the Advisory Committee recommended *against* was a plan to close the Westlake Village Golf Course, to change the zoning from Highway-Commercial to Recreational-Commercial, and to permit development on the site of a hotel, an office complex, and a shopping center—and the Council agreed with the recommendation!

After more than thirteen months of effort at seventeen well-attended meetings, the Citizen's Advisory Committee was disbanded with the sincere appreciation of the Council for the extensive efforts and time the members had dedicated to the important General Plan project.

In accordance with state mandate, a full review of the General Plan was conducted in 1991. The City Council again appointed a twenty-eight-member Citizen's Advisory Committee to participate with and guide the Plan contractor. Many Committee members were the same as those who had served in 1982–1983 (Appendix C), and again the contractor selected was Envicom, Inc.

By 1991, state requirements had been modified to require the General Plan to address only seven elements:

Conservation	Circulation
Open Space	Safety
Land Use	Noise
Housing	

Reports subsequent to a General Plan submittal are now limited to the Housing Element, and at five-year intervals. These reports are sent to the State Department of Housing and Community Development, which has a forty-five-day period in which to comment or certify. The City's Housing Element update of 1990 was reviewed and certified, but no submittal was required in 1995 due to lack of state personnel. The city submitted a Year 2000 Housing Element update and responded to state comments.

With the realization that most of the city's citizens looked favorably on their performance during the difficult initial year, the Council members entered their second year with confidence and enthusiasm.

Particularly pleasing was the January Audit Report, which not only confirmed that the city was in sound financial condition, but that over $500,000 was on deposit in special high interest accounts—earning from 8 percent to 10.25 percent.

Another January report by an intern working at City Hall indicated that 582 businesses were operating in the city ranging from large concerns with several hundred employees to one-person businesses being operated from home.

In February, the Council for the first time approved the installation of a traffic light at the Thousand Oaks Boulevard and Lindero Canyon Road intersection. The cost of $90,000 to $95,000 was to be recovered in the future from developer fees and the completion date was scheduled for August.

Other city activities included approval by the Citizens Advisory Committee—and referral to the Council—of the Westlake Pointe condominium project.

THE REST OF THE 1980s

The Westlake Women's Club donated $6,700 for plants to help beautify the Westlake Boulevard-101 Freeway interchange. In return, CALTRANS agreed to pay for the installation of an irrigation system and work was started in April.

In June, the Council approved an '83-'84 budget of $1.9 million, which included $9,000 to cover a $150 per-month salary for each Council member. That salary issue, while favorably viewed by most city residents, generated concern among a small group. Later, that group obtained a restriction passed by the voters, which prohibited the Council from ever increasing their emolument without approval of the electorate. (Some time later, a state law was passed, which permitted a monthly salary up to $300, where it remains in 2002.)

The city received a formal application in early July requesting a zone change and a General Plan amendment to permit commercial development of the golf course site. The City Council responded by requiring an EIR to address such issues as noise, pollution, aesthetics, and traffic with the estimated cost of $48,580 to be paid by Westlake Village Associates (a Ludwig company). A contract for the EIR was placed with Michael Brandman and Associates for preparation and completion of the report by October—with the proviso that it be based on Westlake Village Associates' finalized plans—which in late August were still some weeks away.

In July, the Council hired Wildan Associates to perform the city's engineering functions at $800 per month and that relationship has continued successfully well into 2002 (although the fee has changed).

Partially because of Proposition 13, passed in 1978, the state's '83–'84 budget faced a $1.5 billion shortfall. At that time a state law existed which required counties to share a portion of property taxes with cities. Under Governor Deukmejian, a part of certain specific property taxes imposed by state law were proposed to be no longer shared with cities which had incorporated after Proposition 13 became law. The result to Westlake Village would have been a reduction of income by $120,000. The Westlake Village City Council took a lead role in opposing that action through State Senator Edward M. Davis's bill, SB165, introduced in Sacramento. After Mayor Berniece Bennett, Mayor Pro Tem Franklin Pelletier, and City Manager James Emmons testified on the bill, it was ultimately passed insuring that such funds would continue to flow to cities. The Westlake Village City Council was recognized as the driving force in keeping such income flowing to cities.

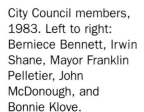

City Council members, 1983. Left to right: Berniece Bennett, Irwin Shane, Mayor Franklin Pelletier, John McDonough, and Bonnie Klove.

In October, a decision taken by the City Council negated a proposal to extend Triunfo Canyon Road eastward past the Oak Forest Mobile Home Estates to the City of Westlake Village-Los Angeles County line, thus providing a direct link to Kanan Road. Proponents of the extension cited advantages of another exit route in event of a disaster as well as easier access to beach areas, but the Council recognized that Triunfo Canyon could become a "bypass" route for through traffic when the 101 Freeway became clogged and voted it down.

The city's new General Plan, the result of over twenty months of effort by the Citizens Advisory Committee, was finally adopted in November—more than a year before state law required it.

In December, the next rotational change of leadership took place when Franklin Pelletier succeeded Berniece Bennett as mayor.

1984

The year started with an agreement that the city needed an emergency plan to insure some level of support for its residents in event of a disaster. A previous booklet on emergency information was considered outdated, so the Council determined a new and up-to-date version was needed. To implement that action, the Council appointed a

Westlake Village Preparedness Committee to review needs, make recommendations, and generate a new booklet. On January 11, each of the Council members appointed four citizens to serve on that committee. (Appendix G)

When the Las Virgenes Municipal Water District announced its plans in March to build a filtration plant at the top of the Westlake Dam, they also advised no public access would be permitted to the area despite the agreement reached when American-Hawaiian donated the site for the dam plus $1 million. That agreement provided access by the public to the reservoir for boating and fishing, but not for swimming.

National Bulk Carriers, a corporation owned by the founder of the Westlake Village development and multi-billionaire Daniel K. Ludwig, had announced its plan to close the Westlake Village Golf Course and convert the property to commercial use. The claim was made that no commitment had ever been made to homebuyers to keep the golf course in operation forever and that it was losing money. The Council considered ways that the city might be able to acquire the property, but none appeared viable.

In mid-April, Westlake Village Associates (WVA), a Ludwig successor company set up to handle the golf course and properties north of the freeway surrounding the cemetery, met with City Manager James Emmons and City Planning Director Rick Vena to obtain guidance on procedures for submittal of plans for the developments. Eleven days later the Westlake Joint Board appointed a five-member citizen's committee to generate information for use in opposing such changes.

In May, the Council was asked to approve a car wash/gasoline station at the northwest corner of the Thousand Oaks Boulevard–Lindero Canyon Road intersection. Considerable protest was heard from residents in Westlake Canyon Oaks since the operation would be within two hundred yards of some residences. Some claims were made of deed restrictions that would negate such use, but the document was never produced. After some modifications to the design and consideration of some other types of operations that might be permitted under the property's commercial designation and despite the receipt of a 239-signature petition from the Westlake Joint Board of Homeowners Associations, the car wash was approved.

At the same meeting, the Council also approved the sixty-four-unit condominium to be known as Westlake Pointe, with some assurance that blasting on the site might not be required (but was later found to be necessary).

Also in May, the Council took action to honor the first and second mayors of the city by naming the City Council chambers after John H. McDonough and changing the name of Reyes Park to Bennett Park after Berniece Bennett. In that same month, the city officials were pleased to learn that to date the city's income exceeded the estimate in the '83–'84 budget by $150,000.

The very first—and only—performance of the Westlake Village Symphony was presented in July by the Westlake Village Cultural Foundation. The concert, conducted by Walter Moeck, was held in the auditorium at the Calvary Community Church on Via Colinas. Even though the performance

Right: Berniece Bennett Park. (Courtesy Lussier Photography)

received very favorable local comment, the gate receipts fell far short of the costs, and no further concerts were planned.

The city adopted a Blasting Ordinance in early September to control any blasting and potentially subsequent damage that might result from such activity on the Westlake Pointe site.

In that same month, Griffin Homes, then building affordable condominiums just across the Los Angeles–Ventura County line in the Thousand Oaks part of Westlake Village, offered $10,000 to Westlake Canyon Oaks Homeowner's Association for a plot of land at the northeast corner of Thousand Oaks Boulevard and Via Colinas. The developer planned to landscape that area, which was at the entrance to his development. Westlake Canyon Oaks countered with an asking price of $50,000. The deal was finalized at an undisclosed sum.

McCoy Land and Investment Company presented to the Council a proposal to build 484 townhomes in late September. These units were to be located east of and down the slope from the reservoir. Jim D. Johnson, formerly with American-Hawaiian and Westlake's very first resident, was the principal owner of the company. That same proposal came before the Council at a later time, but was not approved and was eventually abandoned.

On October 10, Westlake Village Associates requested that the Council postpone action on a Council-planned survey of city residents on the golf course proposal, and to table their request for conversion at least until January of 1985. However, WVA launched a major publicity blitz in early November to promote its position with the public. At a meeting held in the Westlake Plaza Hotel, the estimated four hundred attendees almost unanimously expressed opposition to the golf course conversion, even though WVA's attorney, Allen Camp, is quoted in the press as saying, "I know you want the golf course to stay, but folks, that is not going to happen." It was noted that Camp had previously stated if the WVA proposal for conversion was not approved, the golf course would be closed down.

City historians Ray and Joyce Prouty.

39

November also saw Doris Rufener appointed as the first city historian, a position in which she developed the programs—still in use today—to record and file all significant items in the operations of the city, as well as nongovernmental issues of interest to the community. After almost four years of building up the city's historical records, Mrs. Rufener was succeeded in her efforts by Joyce and Ray Prouty, who at the end of 2002 are still devoting their time to keeping the city's historical files current.

In late November, then Mayor Berniece Bennett and Mayor Pro Tem Franklin Pelletier along with City Attorney Michael Jenkins traveled to New York for a meeting with Ludwig. After protracted discussions with Ludwig and his staff he agreed to delay closure of the golf course as long as the city was "open and candid" in its discussions with his company.

After many months of dedicated effort by the members of the Westlake Village Preparedness Committee (as well as the Council members) the city's new Emergency Handbook was ready in November 1984. Corporate sponsors paid $6,000 for the four thousand copies, which were mailed out to every residence and business in the city, as well as to all real estate offices in the area.

Also in late 1984, Beautification Chairman Delores Simon of the Westlake Village Women's Club announced donations received for the landscape beautification of the Lindero Canyon Road–101 Freeway interchange—$3,750 from Gibraltar Savings and Loan plus another $1,900 from individuals and local businesses. Despite the difficulties of working with CALTRANS (the state highway agency), the project was sufficiently impressive to earn the Beautification Award from the National Federation of Women's Clubs.

Regina Sheil (left), Miss Westlake Village 1983, and Mary Elva Anderson-Lussier (right), Chamber president 1984, at Westlake Village Chamber of Commerce Expo 1984.

Owners of the Westlake Village Riding Club, located on nearly five acres below the Westlake Lake Dam on the site now occupied by The Cove, applied to the city for permission to build a ninety-thousand-square-foot facility on the site. Two buildings were proposed—a two-story office building and a three-story office and restaurant complex with a fifty-two-foot tower. After first rejecting the proposal, the Council approved a modified version in mid-December.

December saw the usual "changing of the guard" on the City Council when Mayor Franklin Pelletier turned over the gavel to the new mayor, Irwin Shane.

In January, the Council approved the McCoy Land and Investment Company's revised proposal for a 428-multiple-family-home community, to be jointly developed with WSLA Development Company. Plans for this new "Westlake View" gate-guarded development called for some homes to overlook the reservoir, and others to have a lake view.

Less than five months after the mayor and mayor pro tem received assurance from D. K. Ludwig that the golf course would not be closed as long as open dialogue continued with his

41

Aerial view of Westlake Village Golf Course. (Courtesy Walter Dibble, Photographic Illustrator)

company, the situation changed radically. Two nights, March 27 and 28, saw the Westlake Village Associates back before the Council, again requesting a zone change to permit commercial development of the golf course and additionally to allow a high density residential development on twenty-six acres north of the Valley Oaks Cemetery. When Council members questioned the WVA representative's claim that the golf course had never been built as an inducement to potential homebuyers, the WVA spokesman Allen Camp—according to press reports—protested what he called "allegations of fraud" and stated he "will not entertain future questions of this nature." He was also quoted as saying such questions belonged in a courtroom.

On the green at Westlake Village Golf Course.

One week later, after intensive discussions and deliberation, the Council rejected both proposals.

Another major decision by the Council was to permit Prudential Insurance Company (now the owner of the North Ranch area), to pave the last stretch (less than a half mile) of Lindero Canyon Road, from just north of Hedgewall Drive to the City-Ventura County line thus opening that access to traffic from Oak Park and Thousand Oaks. A bridge proposed to be built over the creek on the east side of Lindero Canyon to allow traffic to also access the freeway via Reyes Adobe Road in Agoura Hills. Prudential offered to pay Agoura Hills the $500,000 cost of the bridge as well as $250,000 to fund improvements to the Reyes Adobe Road-101 Freeway interchange. As another inducement, Prudential offered Westlake Village $400,000 for park development. The Council initially approved the proposal on March 1, but then put it on hold until July 10. The City of Agoura Hills refused Prudential's offers and negated the proposal to connect Reyes Adobe Road to Lindero Canyon Road via the proposed bridge.

In April, the city completed and occupied the new 1,250-square-foot Council chambers in the First Neighborhood building, which brought the total city occupancy to forty-one hundred square feet.

April also saw the filing in federal court of a $1,000,000 lawsuit against the city by the owners of the Oak Forest Mobile Home property. The suit alleged that the city's rent control ordinance in effect created a "taking" under the Fifth Amendment of the U.S. Constitution.

The city had received $26,000 in Revenue Sharing grants from the federal government in February and had appointed a city committee to review applications and make recommendations to the Council on allocation of the funds. (Appendix H) By vote of the Council, those recommendations were ratified in April with about one-half of the funds going to local agencies: Meals on Wheels, Conejo Youth Employment Services, National Charity League, Action for Seniors, Hospice of the Conejo, Westlake Athletic Association, and Westlake Cultural Foundation and half to agencies such as the Las Virgenes Unified School District, Las Virgenes Library, Animal Control, and the local Los Angeles County Sheriff station.

A study was completed in May on Westlake Village's needs for public transportation. Proposition A Transit Funds were used to fund the study, which disclosed that from thirty-five to fifty elderly citizens might have such requirements.

In June, the Memorex division of Burroughs Corporation, the first large

manufacturing operation in Westlake Village, announced the closure of its plant on Lindero Canyon Road. Over six hundred employees were expected to be released over the next few months. Shortly thereafter, Disk Media, Inc., a joint venture of Memorex and Control Data Corporation, announced its plans to phase out its operations over the next few months.

The Council voted in July to adopt a fiscal year '85-'86 budget of $2,891,195.

The need for widening the Lindero Canyon Road Bridge below the Westlake Lake Dam had been studied by the Council for some time and in September the decision was reached to proceed with the project.

In October, Congress decided to eliminate Federal Revenue Sharing Funds from the 1986-1987 federal budget, leaving it up to cities to fund their own programs of allocations to local organizations.

Nineteen eighty-five was an election year—the first since the city was founded and the original Council elected in 1981. Only three seats were open, those of Klove, Shane, and Pelletier, all of whom decided to run for reelection. Only one nonincumbent filed—Anthony Plaia, a long-term resident of First Neighborhood. Despite an active campaign by Plaia, including some television ads produced at the local studios of Storer Cable, he was defeated

City Council members, 1985. Left to right: Franklin Pelletier, Berniece Bennett, Mayor Bonnie Klove, Irwin Shane, and Mayor Pro Tem John McDonough.

by a margin of only nine votes. The final vote counts were:

Pelletier	972
Klove	957
Shane	810
Plaia	801

On December 5, Bonnie Klove was selected by the Council to serve as the city's mayor for the upcoming year, and John McDonough was elected mayor pro tem.

1986

The year was to see many requests for approval of development projects—residential, business park, and commercial—which required much staff time and in-depth study by the Council members.

In January, the Las Virgenes District School Board deferred plans for sale of their acreage between Foxfield Drive and Oak Ranch Court.

The Council approved funding for landscaping and equipping a two-acre park in Westlake Canyon Oaks, to be known as Canyon Oaks Park. Work on constructing the new park was expected to start in the late spring.

After considerable study, the Council decided to follow the recommendations of the city manager and city treasurer to computerize the city's financial records. Some Council members, while agreeing that computer word processing had proven successful, still had some concerns about committing all city financial record keeping to an unproved system. An agreement was reached to do both hand and computer recording for a brief period until the latter proved acceptable.

Early in the year a total of $37,958 in Federal Revenue Sharing Funds became available and the Council again activated a citizens committee to evaluate requests and to make recommendations on allocation. (Appendix H) The several agencies eligible to participate were notified, with applications due on January 31. Groups such as Meals on Wheels, Interface, etc., shared $18,460 and government agencies—Sheriff and Fire Departments, and others—received $18,498.

Canyon Oaks Park
dedication.

The Southern California Rapid Transit District (RTD) announced in January their plans to eliminate the two bus lines serving Westlake Village and Agoura Hills. The situation developed when Congress proposed a $5 million cut in RTD funding. The two cities threatened to pull out of the agency, taking their allocation of $900,000 with them. In response, the RTD planning director stated that the RTD would fight any such action. The affected bus lines were No. 161, Canoga Park to Westlake Village, scheduled for an almost immediate termination on January 26 and No. 423, Westlake Village to downtown Los Angeles, on July 1. Alternatives were studied by the Council, including establishment of a regional bus system in partnership with Thousand Oaks. At the request of the two cities, Assemblywoman Cathie Wright sponsored a bill, AB3159,

that would permit them to pull out of the system. State Senator Ed Davis also promised support. The expected federal cuts were delayed, so the RTD put off any cuts until late March. Then on February 22, the RTD staff recommended to their Board to delay any shutdown until June 30. Ultimately, funding was found and neither of the lines was eliminated. The cities asked Assemblywoman Wright to withdraw her bill—with thanks for her support.

When in February it was disclosed that the city had a $2.5 million surplus, the Council agreed to study ways in which the funds could be returned to the taxpayers.

On March 14, the Three Springs development—the preliminary tract map and conditional use permit, which had been approved by the county prior to cityhood—came before the Council. The plan called for 481 single-family homes in the range of twenty-four hundred to twenty-six hundred square feet. A Planned Development Permit was approved by the Council with some modifications, including the construction of a 6.2-acre passive park.

A ninety-day trial of a new Dial-A-Ride program was approved on April 16. Under a contract with the Thousand Oaks Cab Company, the city was to provide transportation twenty-four hours a day to any point within a four-mile radius for $1.00, subsidized by Proposition A funds. Service started on May 1 and was found to be used by a number of residents with no alternative means of transportation. Soon trips to Los Robles Hospital were added at $3.00 each way. Ultimately, the program was deemed successful, and became a permanent service. On August 18, the Council voted to reduce cost for local trips to fifty cents although Los Robles runs stayed at $3.00.

The city gave final approval on May 14 to Kaiser Development Company for a $65 million business park on fifty-five acres along the south side of Agoura Road, just east of Lindero Canyon Road. The original plan called for a total building construction area of 526,000 square feet, but was scaled down to 420,000 square feet by the Council. As part of the agreement, Kaiser gave the county a two-acre plot also known as Lot 9, at the southeast corner of Agoura Road and Oak Crest Drive on which to build a library, with the proviso that if the county did not start construction by December 31, 1986, the property would belong to the city. (Ultimately, the county did not take that action, so the property reverted to city ownership.) Additionally, Kaiser dedicated to the city a 2.6-acre, open-space preserve essentially surrounding the building sites. Because a considerable increase in traffic was expected from the development, Kaiser was assessed $150,000 for improvements at the Kanan Road–101 Freeway interchange, and another $30,000 to be put into the city's traffic signal fund.

May saw the start of another commercial development at the northeast corner of Lindero Canyon Road and Thousand Oaks Boulevard when the Council approved the North Ranch Gateway Shopping Center. It was to be anchored by a 33,430-square-foot Hughes Market. Two other store buildings were included, all designed by Benton Park/Candreva. Part of the agreement with the developer was payment to the city of $100,000 for improvements along Thousand Oaks Boulevard and $22,500 for traffic signals.

A committee was set up by the Council to advise on disposition of city income declared excess under the Gann Act. In May, the committee, recognizing the limit had been set too low by LAFCO at the city's incorporation, recommended an override election be held—as permitted by law—to permit retention of that excess.

At the request of many of the city's youths, a Proposition A subsidized beach bus service to Zuma Beach was started on June 19, at a cost of fifty cents each way and the program ran through August 3.

Prudential Development Company submitted a plan to the city in July for opening up the Yellowwood and Montview Court cul-de-sacs to accommodate traffic from a new-gated development planned for construction on the Thousand Oaks side of the county line. It was claimed that the forty-six to forty-eight gated homes on half-acre plots, to be built in a bowl-shaped property, would require those two accesses through the city to meet safety requirements. Residents in the Three Springs area protested strongly against granting such access, citing the noise, truck and construction equipment traffic, and dirt that would be generated on their streets during a year or more of construction and the increased traffic through their area after construction was completed. The Council voted unanimously to reject the request.

At the first Council meeting in July the city adopted an fiscal year '86–'87 budget of $3.4 million, and at the second meeting it was voted to increase Council member salaries from $150 to $300 per month, as permitted by state law.

The Council took precautionary action in July to forestall a problem that had occurred in a neighboring community. An ordinance was adopted prohibiting waitresses or female entertainers from displaying "any portion of either breast below a straight line" drawn between the nipples.

In September, the city shared in the distinction of having White Oak Elementary School recognized as one of only 272 elementary schools in the entire nation to be honored under the National Elementary School Program. Betty DeSantis, chairman of the Las Virgenes Unified School Board, accompanied Principal Rene Lamkay, teacher Mildred Berge of White Oak, and Dr. Albert Marley, the district superintendent, on their visit to Washington, D.C. At a reception in the White House, President Ronald Reagan praised their accomplishments. They were also presented with an "Excellence in Education" flag by the U.S. Department of Education and in November that flag was raised at White Oak School.

From September 16 to Veterans Day in November the first showing of a one-half scale replica of the Vietnam Veterans Memorial was on display at Valley Oaks Memorial Park.

Pierce Brothers Valley
Oaks Cemetery.
(Courtesy Lussier
Photography)

In October it was determined that the city had an estimated surplus of $2.6 million. Suggestions were made by the Council to return the money to the city's residents. After considerable review, no equitable means for such distribution could be determined, so no further action was taken.

A report from the state received in October indicated the city income had exceeded the state-imposed Gann limit for the prior year by $61,355. At their second November meeting the Council voted to return the excess to the taxpayers—after deducting the state's share of $15,000. A decision on method of distribution was deferred until 1987.

Near the end of the year, the Las Virgenes Unified School District announced plans to sell the nineteen-acre Foxfield-to-Oak Ranch Court site, which had been purchased from American-Hawaiian in 1968 for

$590,000. St. Jude's Catholic Church indicated an interest in purchasing five acres of the site, next to the fire station for church parking, but a special city planner retained to review the specific site recommended it be used for city and school district offices and thirty-nine single-family homes in one-third-acre lots.

In December the Council selected the city's first mayor, John H. McDonough, to again serve in that position for the coming year.

1987

The year opened with the revelation that the city's income would exceed the state-imposed Gann limit by $75,502 at the middle of the fiscal year. If no other legal use of the funds were implemented by June, the monies would have to be turned over to the state by July 1. At the second January meeting, the Council agreed to study the issue in more detail prior to determining the action to be taken.

Despite the severe concerns of some citizens—particularly about potential damage to the reservoir dam—and after considerable study and expert advice, the Council approved a blasting permit in January for the Three Springs tract. The contractor advised that some dense pockets of rock were resistant to even the heaviest construction equipment.

In order to prepare for the possibility of further Gann limit problems, the Council decided to establish a Gann Limit Committee to study the problems, review the available options, and file a report and recommendations with the city. Each Council member appointed two residents and hired a consultant to work with the Committee. (Appendix I) Jim D. Johnson was appointed chairman of the group, and David De Roos of Arthur Young and Company was retained as the staff consultant compensated from an $18,500 budget established by the Council. The first two meetings of the group were held April 1 and 16, with five more scheduled if required. The final recommendation to the Council was to put the issue on the ballot, as permitted by law, for the electorate to decide whether to keep the funds or return them to the state and to return the current excess funds to the residents of the city.

In mid-March the Los Angeles County Planning Commission was presented with a proposal to build a luxury health spa in Triunfo Canyon, east of the Oak Forest Mobile Home Estates. The location proposed was just outside of city limits in a county-controlled area. The plans called for $23 million in construction and included over ninety-six thousand square feet of buildings—a two-story,

thirty-three-thousand-square-foot main building, nine smaller buildings each with ten luxury guest rooms, nine parking lots, and a large swimming pool. It was estimated that 119 employees would serve the expected 126 guests. The applicant claimed to have invested several hundred thousands of dollars with planners, architects, and others. Ultimately the county rejected the proposal.

An unfortunate incident occurred in late March when a vandal set a fire in the ladies room at City Hall. Over $2,000 worth of damage ensued and the fire jeopardized the entire building.

The "Foxfield site" as it came to be known, had been sold by the school district and was scheduled for development. In early April, Council action was taken to approve rezoning of the property to permit construction of thirty-three homes on the nineteen acres. Lots were to be from fifteen to twenty-two thousand square feet. Additionally, 1.3 acres were set aside next to the Fire Station for "public purposes" such as a City Hall, or other government services, with the proviso that if no such planning occurred within ten years, the ownership would revert to the school district.

On April 19, the owners of the Oak Forest Mobile Home Estates filed a lawsuit against the city in federal court, asking $1 million in damages. A violation of the Fifth Amendment to the Constitution was alleged—a "taking" of the owners interests by reducing land values while increasing resale value of the renters' coaches. At about the same time, the Council refused to take action to rescind the ordinance as requested by a 662-signature petition.

The city had been operating with a part-time planner under a contract with Los Angeles County. In early May it was decided that the workload justified a full-time position. Robert Theobald, who had held the part-time job, accepted the city's offer and became the city's planner and ultimately the planning director—a position he still holds in 2002.

With the city's Rent Control Ordinance due to expire by June 30, the Council voted 3-2 to extend it— McDonough and Bennett dissenting. Councilman Pelletier announced that he planned to introduce an ordinance that would extend such rent control indefinitely.

Also in May, the Council authorized renewal of the Sheriff's Department contract at $805,000 for fiscal year '87–'88.

In early June, after twenty years as a landmark operation in Westlake Village, the Westlake Village Riding Club moved its horses (and one steer) to its new location in Thousand Oaks.

A $3.8 million budget for fiscal year '87–'88 was adopted by the Council on June 10. At that same meeting Consultant David De Roos reported the Gann Committee's recommendations. First, the current Gann excess of $75,602 should be returned to the taxpayers. Secondly, a question should be put on the upcoming ballot for voters to decide if Gann excesses over the next four years should be returned to the state or retained by the city.

Mid-June saw the opening of discussions between the city's planning director and Carlton Brown—the development arm of Westlake Village Associates—on plans for the 129 acres of open land surrounding the cemetery.

In late June the Council voted unanimously to follow the recommendations of the Gann Committee: return the current Gann excess of $75,595 to the taxpayers, via a reduction in landscaping and street lighting assessments (about $22 for each residence and slightly more for businesses). On a 4-1 vote it was agreed to put the issue of Gann excesses on the upcoming ballot. Under state law if the measure were passed it would permit city retention of those excess funds for four years (1985-1989). Further recommendations were for the city to seek legislation in Sacramento to allow cities incorporated after Gann became law to have their limits reviewed and raised, or to have another override vote by the taxpayers in 1989 or 1990.

In early July, the Council followed the Gann Committee recommendation and voted to put the issue to the voters in the upcoming November 3 election. Also in July, the Council contracted with McClelland Engineering Company to conduct an environmental impact study (EIR) on a Prudential Insurance Company proposal to build a 260-dwelling-unit community and a small shopping area on sixty-four acres of open land on a downslope south of the Three Springs development. Cost of the EIR was $55,750, to be reimbursed by the applicant.

Early in August the residents of The Colony were startled when a naked twenty-seven-year-old Westlake Village man broke into three residences. He was apprehended with little disturbance, and no losses were reported.

Plans were under way for the construction in Thousand Oaks of a building to house the many human services that were serving the area including the people in the City of Westlake Village. To be known as "Under One Roof," it would accommodate fifteen thousand square feet of offices for agencies such as Social Security, Hospice of the Conejo, Action for Seniors, Conejo Youth Employment Services, Many Mansions, and others. After a full review, the Council determined that Community Development Block Grant monies from Los Angeles County would qualify for

such use and contributed $50,000 to the effort—the city's first usage of such funds.

On July 15, the Council voted the largest funding to date for traffic signalization at the Lindero Canyon Road–101 Freeway interchange.

It was election year again and in July, Berniece Bennett, Kenneth Rufener, and Tony Plaia took out papers declaring themselves candidates for the two Council seats that would be open. Two issues would also be on the ballot. If passed, Measure X was an override that would permit the city to keep funds collected in excess of the Gann limit for the next four years (estimated at over $682,000 from fiscal year '85–'86 through fiscal year '88–'89). Measure Z, placed on the ballot by a citizens group, would prevent any future City Council from raising their salaries (then, as now, at $300 per month), or expense account budget without a vote of the electorate. A proposal had been considered to place Measure Y on the ballot to abolish rent control at the Mobile Home Park. However the $1 million lawsuit against the city was dropped in an agreement that allowed the tenants to buy their lots, so the issue was not included on the ballot.

In late July, the community was shocked when a body was discovered in the decorative pond at the back of the Westlake Inn. It later turned out to be that of a twenty-three-year-old Westlake Village male.

In what was to turn out as the final year of Federal Revenue Sharing, in July the Allocation Committee (Appendix H) recommended the following distribution of the funds:

Non-Profit Groups

Interface $1,500
Hospice of the Conejo $1,500
Livingston Visiting
      Nurses $1,250
Westlake Village
      Meals on Wheels $1,500
Action for Seniors $800
Agoura Chargers Club $800
Westlake Village
      Chamber of Commerce . . $834
Conejo Youth
      Employment Service $800
Westlake Village
      Cultural Foundation $750
Villa Esperanza $600
Conejo Community
      Services $500
Village Voices $210
Conejo Symphony
      Orchestra $500

Government Groups

Animal Control $4,421
      (for all-terrain vehicle)
Fire Department $1,800
      (for two emergency
      electric generators)

Las Virgenes Library $900
      (for computerized
      cataloging system)
Las Virgenes Unified
      School District $4,050
      (for White Oak Elementary
      School handball court)
Sheriff's Department $1,132
      (for Neighborhood and
      Business Watch programs)

Confidential negotiations between the mobile home park owners and the city had been ongoing since the spring, following shortly after the filing of the lawsuit in federal court. Despite rumors that the sale of lots to the renters in the mobile home park was being discussed seriously, owners of the park stated in mid-July that negotiations had stalled. They claimed it was caused by the city's demands that the park owners must first build a secondary access road and because no decision had been reached on who should handle negotiations for the residents. The talks had included tentative agreements to provide for sale of the lots to the renters, to hold any further rent increases to 75 percent of increases in the Consumer Price Index, but not to exceed 15 percent in any one year until rents were at "fair market" levels of comparable parks. Those who chose to purchase their lots were to be offered certain inducements such as thirty-year mortgages at market rates for those who could not otherwise qualify. Those who opted to leave and take their coaches were offered $7,500 to help defray the expense. Other inducements were also proposed. After other discussions, another closed meeting started on September 2. After a marathon session, final agreements were reached in the early hours of the next morning— just two weeks before the scheduled court date for the federal lawsuit.

Also included in the agreement was rescision of the city's rent control ordinance, to be replaced by one similar to the county's ordinance, permanent rent decontrol when a coach was sold in place to a new owner and permission for the park owners to develop thirty-five more lots, with agreed timetables for submittal of a subdivision map. Other results of the agreement were elimination from the upcoming November ballot of Measure Y—a vote by the electorate on the rent control ordinance—and a request to the appointed federal judge to approve the agreement.

In mid-October the Council authorized issuance of $1.1 million in bonds to finance the widening of the bridge at the end of Lindero Canyon Road. An assessment district was created to retire the bonds, with assessments of $948 per dwelling unit for the 481 to be built at Three Springs, 64 homes planned for the downslope south of Three Springs, and varying fees for the commercial

developments planned for the Borges former stable property.

October 16 was the opening date for the new Canyon Oaks Park. Originally scheduled for completion in July at an estimated cost of $101,000, changes, additional features, and delays ran the costs to $118,000 and added three months to the schedule. The Westlake Women's Club donated two oak trees, which were planted on the opening date. Lee Newman Landscape Associates directed design of the park.

At the October 21 meeting, the Council formally approved a General Plan amendment and a zone change to permit the increase of lots at the Oak Forest Mobile Home Estates from 162 to 197, and at the same meeting rejected a proposal to increase commercial space at The Landing by eighteen thousand square feet.

In late October, the Eaton Corporation announced plans to sell off its defense electronic businesses, including its Information Management Systems Division on La Tienda Drive. Eleven hundred employees were to be released by the closure of that facility.

In early November, a group of residents in the mobile home park sought to block growth at that location by having the Council rescind the approval of thirty-five more lots. That action would have placed the agreement with the park owners in jeopardy and was eventually rejected.

November 3 was Election Day. Two Council seats were open and two measures were also on the ballot. Berniece Bennett and Kenneth Rufener were the winners, while both Measures X and Z were approved. Measure X, which permitted the city to keep any Gann excess income, passed overwhelmingly and Measure Z requiring a vote of the electorate to change Council salaries also won, by an almost two-to-one margin. For a limited local election, the voter turnout of 37 percent was considered very satisfactory. Total vote counts were:

Bennett	1,130
Rufener	880
Plaia	703

	Yes	No
Measure X	1,160	236
Measure Z	945	485

In late November, Mayor John McDonough gave a State of the City address at a dinner attended by a large number of residents. He stressed the city's excellent financial condition and the low-key approach to governing followed by all City Councils since the city's inception.

On December 2, Berniece Bennett was elected mayor by her fellow Council members. Franklin Pelletier was selected as mayor pro tem, and Kenneth Rufener was sworn in as the newest Council member.

The city turned down the federal government on December 11 when the Council refused to extend the tract

City Council members, 1987. Left to right: Kenneth Rufner, Bonnie Klove, Mayor Pro Tem Franklin Pelletier, Mayor Berniece Bennett, and Irwin Shane. (Courtesy Lussier Photography)

filing date for 441 condominiums—the former McCoy Land Investment Company project near the reservoir. The sequence of events involved was all too typical of the times. McCoy had sold the development project in August 1986 to the M. D. Janes Company, which had financed the deal with a loan from Vernon Savings and Loan. Vernon closed shop in March 1987 and the federal agency, Federal Savings and Loan Insurance Company (FSLIC), took over the operation. FSLIC then contracted with another government agency, the Federal Asset Disposition Association to manage the property. The FADA in turn contracted with Pacific Rim Associates to continue the development effort. Despite the federal government's claim that ten major companies were interested in buying the property and continuing with its development, the City Council denied the requested one-year extension for tract filing. Many citizens who had become opposed to the project lauded that decision.

In late December, the Kaiser Development Company sold their interest in the fifty-five-acre site along Agoura Road to Bedford Properties. Thereafter the commercial site was to be known as Westlake Spectrum.

In early January the Council reviewed two petitions signed by 507 registered voters. The petitions, which had been initiated by residents on the Ridge, requested that 1) the Council rescind the agreement to allow thirty-five more lots in the Mobile Home Park, and 2) that the agreement to sell lots to the tenants also be rescinded. These items were then scheduled to be put on the ballot at a special election in April as Measure A. With a surprisingly high turnout of 34 percent of voters, the requests to invalidate the agreements were defeated 822 to 544. An interesting aspect of the campaign preceding the vote was that the park owners and the renters worked together to bring about the result they both wanted—sale of the lots.

January was also the month that the North Ranch Gateway Partnership purchased from Watt Industries (developer of the Westlake Canyon Oaks tract) an open section of land, designated Lot 79, for a reported price of $165,000. The partners were listed as Robert Bogle, Richard J. Barich, and John McDonough. In the recording of the property, prior to incorporation of the city, the County of Los Angeles had retained to itself any rights to build on the property thus denying them to Watt Industries, which effectively deemed it open space.

Because of continually increasing traffic, the decision had been reached to widen the Lindero Canyon Road–101 Freeway Bridge. A contract for $738,043 was placed with A-C Construction Company in February, with estimated completion in September. A proposal for a new development in the south end of the city was brought to the Council in February by Prudential Insurance Company to be known as "Sherwood Towne." The plan called for construction on a slope north of Decker Canyon Road of thirty-eight high-density apartments (with a total of 108 units), sixteen cottages for seniors, eighty-six single-family homes, and a twenty-thousand-square-foot commercial center—including a gasoline station. Immediate protests were heard, especially from the residents and developers in the Three Springs tract who cited the considerable traffic that would be result on Kirsten Lee Drive and Three Springs Drive. Estimates from the EIR, prepared by McClelland Engineering, indicated the development as planned would generate 3,679 vehicle trips per day. An analysis made the claim that some Three Springs homes would see one vehicle pass every six seconds for ten hours each day. It was also determined that CALTRANS did not plan to improve Decker Canyon Road (State Route 23). Their rationale was that it would have to undergo vast improvements to bring

the road up to full highway standards. Since the property was zoned for ninety residences, a zone change would be required to permit the proposed construction. Additionally, the proposal would result in the removal of eighty-nine mature oak trees. It was rejected.

Early March saw the rebirth of interest in Adult Education classes—with Irwin Shane again the moving force. The Westlake Village Women's Club, under Doris Rufener, sponsored a wide variety of classes. Members assisted with teacher orientation and acted as monitors for a number of the courses. Irwin Shane, the motivator and organizer of the efforts, was named the educational director of the operations. Any profits from the operations were to be divided—75 percent to the Women's Club and 25 percent to the Westlake Village Cultural Foundation. An eight-week program on wines was held at White Oak Elementary School. Other courses included real estate, with eleven speakers in the eight-week course. Eight two-hour seminars were held on equity investments and eight gourmet cooking classes were held at St. Jude's with chefs from top hotels, clubs, and restaurants. Courses in bridge, aerobics, art, golf, and interior design were also available, as well as one on wills, trusts, and taxes.

The Council gave tentative approval in March to construction of three additional two-story office buildings at The

Landing, with the proviso that neither lake views from other properties nor the view of the Yacht Club be impaired.

A preliminary proposal was submitted to the City Council in late March that was the initial effort in what was to become Westlake North. Charles Fry, executive vice president of Carlton Brown and Company—the development arm of Westlake Village Associates—presented the plan to the City Council. The 129 acres of open land surrounding the Valley Oaks Memorial Park was to include a 250-room, four-story Marriott Hotel, a seventy-four-acre business park with six- and four-story buildings and underground parking, a thirty-acre shopping center with three-hundred-thousand square feet of retail shops and four hundred apartments. Carlton Brown also noted that it would take about twelve months of effort to prepare and submit a site plan for the Council's consideration. Fry also advised the Council, "We plan to continue the operation of the golf course as it is." In a letter to all city residents, Fry also stated that successful completion of the Westlake North project "will allow us the resources to continue this commitment to support the golf course for many years to come."

(It was noted that Carlton Brown's parent company, Westlake Village Associates, was owned by a consortium of three savings and loan companies—

Southwest Savings of Phoenix, Home Savings of Houston, and American Savings of Salt Lake City—all of which in turn were interests controlled by D. K. Ludwig, the shipping magnate and developer of Westlake Village.)

In mid-April the Council took action to reinstate the position of city historian, a post that had been vacant since the resignation of Doris Rufener. A number of potential candidates were considered and the obvious choice was Joyce and Ray Prouty. They were not only very early residents—First Neighborhood was still being developed when they moved in—but Ray had spent many days hiking through the mountainous area, learning about its terrain and history. He had also written more than one treatise on the subject. The Proutys, after more than fourteen years of meticulous gathering, collating, and filing of materials involved with our city's history, are still actively engaged in that effort. It cannot be repeated often enough—this history could never have been written without their untiring efforts.

The Council in April also rejected the "Sherwood Towne" proposal presented by Prudential, finding it too dense and with too many access problems. The Westlake Village Joint Board of Homeowner Associations had also taken a strong position opposed to that development proposal.

May saw the Council approve the city's first summer recreation program for children from five to twelve years old. A contract was placed with the Conejo Recreation and Parks District for the six-week program to be conducted at White Oak School, at a cost of $16,310.

A wildfire in late May endangered homes in Westlake Canyon Oaks. A number of Cardoza Drive homeowners hosed down their shake roofs to prevent ignition from flying embers. Fortunately, the Fire Departments of both Los Angeles and Ventura Counties got the conflagration under control, and for a time Thousand Oaks Boulevard had to be closed to accommodate the firefighting equipment.

Goodrich-Baas and Associates received approval from the city in mid-June to build two office buildings of 111,459 square feet each on four lots in The Spectrum, located between Oak Crest Lane and Park Terrace Drive. The world headquarters of Pinkerton Security Company, whose history predates the Civil War, currently occupies the southernmost building. (Alan Pinkerton set up a government security operation at the request of President Lincoln, before the founding of the U.S. Secret Service.) Goodrich-Baas also received approval for the construction of a nineteen-thousand-square-foot office building at the corner of Via Rocas and Cedar Valley Drive. Cotton-Belland Associates at a contract price of $43,616 had developed the Environmental Impact Report for both projects.

In June, the Friends of the Westlake Village Library initiated a drive to raise more funding for the proposed new library. Screen and TV actor Robert Young, of "Dr. Welby" fame, and his wife, Elizabeth, were named honorary co-chairmen of the drive.

The Three Springs development was attracting so many potential buyers in July that the Colonnade tract issued priority numbers to potential buyers, with a date on which they were to return. Even without model homes for inspection, the several builders took reservations from 420 potential home-buyers in three hours. The Oakmont Hills tract took names for a lottery to select buyers for their $499,000 to $550,000 homes and had as many as six potential buyers for each house.

The very first (and to date only) murder in the city occurred in early September when the body of a night-shift welder, Daniel Andrada, was discovered in the parking lot at Raypak on Agoura Road. His death was attributed to blunt force injuries as well as gunshot wounds.

In early November a ribbon-cutting ceremony was held to mark the completion of the Lindero Canyon Road Bridge widening.

At the request of the U.S. Postal Service, a federal judge issued a temporary restraining order in early September against a Cedar Valley Drive mail-order company, which effectively halted delivery of any further mail. Many complaints had been received by both the postal service and the Westlake Village Chamber of Commerce about the company's failure to perform as promised after receipt of deposits. Near the end of the month, the judge extended the order another sixty days to give the company time to rectify the problem, which by that time had grown to over seven hundred complaints. The company attributed the problems to the length of time required to process the many requests, and after refunding many of the payments to customers, the stay was lifted by the court.

In late December, the Westlake Village Yacht Club feted a member, Allison Jolly, and her partner, Lynne Jewell, for their gold-medal win in the yachting competition at the Olympic Games in Seoul, South Korea. The two yachtswomen had raised $13,000 locally to help with the expense of their trip.

In the usual end-of-the-year ceremony, Mayor Berniece Bennett turned over the gavel to her successor, Mayor Pro Tem Franklin Pelletier.

Widening of Lindero Canyon Road Bridge over Triunfo Creek below dam.

The Human Services Center in Thousand Oaks, known as "Under One Roof" was officially dedicated in January. It housed four rent-paying government agencies and twenty-four nonprofit agencies that were not charged for their offices—most of them serving citizens of Westlake Village as well as Thousand Oaks.

A single-engine Cessna aircraft, piloted by an obviously pregnant woman who was flying alone, ran out of fuel and tried to make a dead-stick landing on Lindero Canyon Road, just south of the County line. The plane ran off the roadway and flipped over. A passing motorist released the pilot, hanging upside down in her seat harness. After making a cell phone call, the lady got a ride to Westlake Medical Center where she was checked and found to be in excellent condition. Upon returning to the scene, she asked who had been her benefactor—she was not able to recognize him from her original inverted position.

In mid-January—in efforts to enhance services—officials of Westlake Community Hospital announced a series of changes and improvements to the facility. The name was being changed to "Westlake Medical Center," $100,000 was allocated for improvements to the lobby, cafeteria, and stress unit and $250,000 on renovation of the obstetrics and pediatrics areas, including the addition of two private rooms. Also, a Women's Health Center was to be inaugurated with instructional lectures on breast cancer, birth control, and gynecological problems.

At the first meeting in February, the Council considered the two sites being studied for a new public library— the "Foxfield site" directly across from St. Jude's church and the "Bedford site" at Agoura Road and Oak Crest Drive. In view of the turnout of over one hundred Trails residents who opposed the Foxfield site, the Council agreed unanimously on construction of a $3 million library on the Bedford site, with proposed completion in 1991.

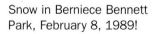
Snow in Berniece Bennett Park, February 8, 1989!

60

In February, Syd Hamilton, owner of Courtesy Chevrolet—the first automobile agency in the new Westlake Village—was named "Man of the Year" by the Westlake Village Chamber of Commerce in recognition of his many contributions to community organizations.

A Housing Element Update Citizen's Advisory Committee was appointed by the Council on March 8, and assigned the task of reviewing and making recommendations on the city's General Plan Housing Element. Their study was to include future expected housing development and conformity with state mandates on affordable housing. (Appendix J)

In early April, the Council dropped plans for a softball field at White Oak Elementary School. Over two hundred signatures on petitions had been received opposing the project and the planned area was found to encroach considerably on First Neighborhood Community Center property as well.

The Cotton-Beland Associates Environmental Impact Report on the Westlake North project was presented to the Council for review on April 20. At that same time, the Council had received letters from both Agoura Hills and Thousand Oaks opposing the project as proposed.

A second Gann Committee was appointed by the Council in mid-April to again recommend to the city disposition of tax funds received in excess of those allowed under state law. (Appendix I)

In the April to June period, the Council studied and took some actions on assault weapons. By a 3–2 vote on April 12, the Council voted a ban on sale or possession of AK47-type weapons, with a second hearing scheduled for May 10. The ordinance would also require that such weapons be turned in to authorities within fifteen days. At the May meeting, the ordinance was passed 3–0 but without the requirement to surrender existing weapons, and with a tie-in to state legislation expected to be signed into law by Governor Deukmejian. On June 14, the Council again voted to restrict sale or possession of such weapons—unless they had been owned prior to June 1 and were registered with the state.

When in May the Council was advised that for some time three residents had been using the subsidized taxi service provided by the city more than fifty times a month, a ruling was adopted that full fare would be charged for any trips exceeding fifty in any month.

In May, the Community Services Funds Allocation Committee made its recommendations to the Council on distribution of $35,074 to a number of local organizations. (Appendix H and H1)

In early May the Council approved two building projects. The first was a seventy-five-thousand-square-foot, three-building complex with an observation tower seventy-five feet high at the former Westlake Riding Club property below the lake dam. The second was a thirty-three-home subdivision on nineteen acres at the site sold by Las Virgenes Unified School District located between Foxfield and Blue Meadow Lane—with construction expected to start in two to three months.

A $4.5 million '89–'90 budget was presented for Council consideration in late May.

Because of vandalizing of the restrooms at Bennett Park, the Council voted in late May to hire a patrol guard to check the facilities each evening. At the same meeting a decision was taken to spend some of the available $43,000 for refurbishment of the Tot Lot.

With the complexities of the Westlake North proposal, and the major impacts it would have on the city, the Council in mid-June opted to use a team approach in its evaluations. Assignments were: Mayor Franklin Pelletier and Councilwoman Berniece Bennett—Financial Impacts and Alternatives, Councilmembers Bonnie Klove and Irwin Shane—Analysis of Alternatives, and Councilmembers Berniece Bennett and Kenneth Rufener—Commercial Developments.

Mid-June also saw the completion and dedication of the city's newest park—Three Springs Park—with its basketball courts, open fields, and jogging track.

Three Springs Park.

On June 28, after receiving recommendations from the Gann Committee, the Council voted to put on the ballot the question of retaining the surplus funds or returning them to the state. At the same meeting the Council approved the conceptual plan for an office park at the site of the closed Burroughs facility, with buildings two and three stories in height.

M. J. Brock submitted plans to the Council for a fifty-six-home development on 176 acres in the southwest corner of the city, fronting on Decker Canyon Road.

On July 14, former City Manager James E. Emmons announced his candidacy for City Council at a large gathering at the Westlake Island home of Mr. and Mrs. John Levey. Within a few days, Sybil Nisenholz, president of the Oak Forest Mobile Home Estates, declared her candidacy as well. In early August, Councilwoman Bonnie Klove also announced her candidacy—for a third term. Douglas R. Yarrow, a resident of Westlake Trails and former president of its association, announced his intent to run for City Council on August 14. With Councilman Irwin Shane and Joanne Robinson also announcing, the slate of six was set to start campaigning.

In July a federal lawsuit almost identical to that brought by owners of the Oak Forest Mobile Home Estates against the city, U.S. District Court Judge Laughlin E. Waters ruled in the plaintiff's favor in *Hall vs. Santa Barbara*. The decision stated in part "The provision that renders this ordinance unconstitutional is the vacancy provision which . . . gives the tenant the possessory interest in Mrs. Hall's property, which consists of the right to occupy the property in perpetuity while paying only a fraction of what it is worth in rent, and which is transferable, and which has an established market and market value." The court also stated "a taking of plaintiff's property has occurred as a result of" the rent control ordinance . . . and the ordinance constitutes taking under the Fifth Amendment." Prior to that ruling, attorneys for the city and Oak Forest owners had been negotiating elements of an equitable settlement, and the court's ruling gave even more impetus to their efforts.

In July, the Council took action on two items involving traffic—parking along both sides of La Tienda within city limits was prohibited, and the Sheriff's Department was authorized to ticket speeders on Three Springs Drive.

August 16 saw the first of many hearings on the Westlake North Environmental Impact Report. Many public comments were received, and final public hearings and, hopefully a vote, were targeted for November. That posed an interesting question: since the

November meeting was scheduled for after the City Council election, should the current Council make the decision on Westlake North before seating the newly elected Council members or leave it for the new group to decide? In response to comments by the Council during the August–November period, the applicant made many changes: reduction in maximum height of buildings from six stories to four, addition of a 4.3-acre park, increase of open areas around buildings, reduction in building areas by forty-five thousand square feet, modified housing from 400 apartments to 250 condominiums, and subsequent reduction in number of mature valley oaks to be removed. Much public comment was received during this period. Many residents of Agoura Hills were vehemently opposed, some preferring the property be left as open space. Letters were received from the Cities of Agoura Hills and Thousand Oaks—mostly in opposition to the project.

Because of complaints from neighbors of Three Springs Park about unacceptable activities in late evenings, the Council on October 10 voted to close the park at 10 p.m. each evening, and requested the Sheriff's Department to monitor compliance. Three Springs residents also requested the city install speed humps along Three Springs Drive, to curb excessive speeding. That request was granted in December.

On October 26 a Candidate's Forum with an attendance of over 120 residents was held at the First Neighborhood Community Center, moderated by the League of Women Voters. The major issue discussed was Westlake North. The candidates brought some of the audience up to date on the latest changes proposed, and expressed their own views on further changes that should be made.

During the campaign, several complaints were lodged about theft of political signs. Such activity is prohibited by law, but unfortunately has continued with each election. In only one instance the culprits were apprehended, charged, and fined by the court.

Election Day was November 7. Results showed the winners of Council seats to be James E. Emmons, Douglas R. Yarrow, and Bonnie Klove. Vote counts were:

Emmons	1,414
Yarrow	1,212
Klove	849
Nisenholz	640
Shane	324
Robinson	264

Also, the vote for the city to retain the excess of Gann Limit funds passed 1,408 to 166.

On November 11, newly elected but not yet seated Council members-elect

Emmons and Yarrow stated they could not approve the Westlake North plans as currently presented. Council member Kenneth Rufener expressed opposition to a delay in the decision until after the new Council members would be seated in December.

The following day, November 12, Westlake Village Associates notified the Council of a further 6 percent reduction being planned for the Westlake North project to better conform to the city's General Plan. The reductions planned were seventy-seven thousand square feet of business park space and nine thousand square feet of shopping area. Other matters, tentatively agreed to in meetings with the Council during the prior week, were a two-hundred-year easement limiting the Westlake Golf Course acreage to open space recreational use, $3.5 million in cash to be paid to the city over seven years after the first building is approved for occupancy, plus $6.5 million for traffic improvements.

The next Council meeting was November 15. Because of the Westlake North issues, a large turnout was expected, and in fact did occur—with over 250 people attending. The Council had arranged for closed circuit television to be shown in the adjacent First Neighborhood Community Center and about 100 people watched the meeting from there. After over thirty speakers had been heard—mostly opposed to the

Westlake North proposal as presented—the decision was made to adjourn the meeting until the following night. One speaker, noting one commercial plot of 150,000 square feet on the plans, had suggested the Council consider reducing that entitlement because it might attract a K-Mart, a Target, or similar "big box" store. (The change was not made, and some years later Price Club/Costco occupied the site.) When the developer's representative was asked if his company would build the four-acre park he advised they would only contribute the raw land. He also advised the $3.5 million donation previously discussed was "off the table." Because of the late hour, the Council agreed to adjourn the meeting.

Mayor Pelletier delivered the State of the City address on November 18, stating that the Westlake North project would be beneficial to the city.

A third hearing on the Westlake North proposal was held on November 28. Almost four more hours of discussions and negotiations ensued, during which City Manager Larry Bagley advised he had received a letter from the Agoura Hills city planner asking that Westlake Village make a contribution of $1.55 million to their city for traffic mitigation. The consensus was then 4-1 in favor of the project as now constituted, with Councilwoman Bennett advising she still saw some "technical problems" needing resolution because two of the three Westlake North owners—out-of-state savings and loans—had been taken over by the federal government. At the close of the meeting Mayor Pelletier made a statement, quoted December 6 in the weekly *Acorn* newspaper as saying, "I don't think in eight years on the City Council I have ever felt more abused by the public."

The December 5 meeting opened with a formal vote on the Westlake North proposal. It was approved 4-1, with Council member Bennett again citing her reservations because of the change in land ownership. Only minutes later, James Emmons and Douglas Yarrow were sworn in and took their seats on the Council dais. Emmons asked for a question session on the Westlake North agreement and was accused by Pelletier of conflict of interest because his company represented a shopping center client across the road from the project. The city attorney did not agree that any such conflict existed.

Bonnie Klove was sworn in December 15 as the city's new mayor. At that same meeting the Council refused a request by the Chabad of the Conejo to display a menorah in the City Hall. The city manager advised that the U.S. Supreme Court had ruled such displays were allowed but not required. Within a week, Mayor Klove reversed that decision and allowed the menorah to be displayed.

1990

It was announced on January 5 by the Agoura Hills City Council that they would not sue the City of Westlake Village for approving the Westlake North project without funding in the Development Agreement for traffic mitigation in their city.

Despite a threatened lawsuit by its proponents, on January 4, the city refused to accept a petition opposing the Westlake North development. The petition was ruled invalid because it did not include the text of the ordinances and resolution that established the project. The city attorney cited two District Court of Appeals decisions to uphold rejection of petitions that "do not comply with a mandatory requirement of the Elections Code and are invalid" and recommended the city return the petition marked "Refused."

In early January, the General Plan Advisory Committee advised it was studying a potential ban on hillside developments within the city. On January 3, the Baldwin Company had submitted its proposal for a mixed single family and condominium development on the property adjacent to the reservoir—on which they had just taken an option from the FDIC in December of 1989. On January 10 the Council decided against freezing of hillside developments. Even though some preliminary study had been made of the Baldwin proposal, on January 25 Baldwin asked that their application be put on temporary hold. Upon withdrawing, Baldwin advised they would agree to abide by the Advisory Committee's recommendations on the number of residences for their development.

In mid-January, the City of Thousand Oaks refused to permit a developer the right to access Highgate Road for his planned Canyon West development and recommended he ask the City of Westlake Village for access through the Three Springs area. The city refused—unless Highgate Road would also be opened. The project was not built.

In mid-February, Baldwin submitted a new proposal showing two marinas on the reservoir to accommodate boats for fishing and recreational boating. They cited the 1970 agreement (to expire in 1999) between the Las Virgenes Municipal Water District and American-Hawaiian, the donor of the property, which provided for recreational use of the reservoir (except swimming), and which also required the Water District to build additional water treatment facilities.

In late February, the Community Service Fund Allocation Committee (Appendix H) presented its recommen-

dations to the Council for the allocation of $42,503 to a number of local organizations. The total of all the requests received for funds was $159,304. The largest allocation recommended was for the Triunfo YMCA—$3,000. The committee also recommended changes in procedures to insure that future allocations would concentrate more on agencies providing services directly to Westlake Village residents.

Despite the Council's November 1989 decision to ban the display of a menorah at City Hall during Hanukkah, a vote was taken in March to reverse that ruling and to accede to the request by the Chabad of the Conejo.

On March 25, the General Plan Advisory Committee advised against approval of the Baldwin project.

Also in late March, City Manager Larry Bagley and Sybil Nisenholz, president of the Oak Forest Mobile Estates Association, traveled to Sacramento to arrange for $1,000,000 in loans to be available to Oak Forest residents to assist in buying their properties in the Park.

In early April, the Los Angeles County Water Board announced it was unsure how long it would be before ground water contamination would be eliminated from the abandoned Burroughs plant site on Lindero Canyon Road. The cleanup of toxic materials had started when Memorex

Right: Summer Knapp celebrating the Fourth of July in Westlake Village. (Courtesy Lussier Photography)

closed the plant four years earlier, and twenty to thirty monitoring wells had been drilled on adjacent properties—even across the Freeway. The Water Board stated however that the amount of contamination found was "a minor quantity."

At the last Council meeting in May it was disclosed that an environmental study of the Lake Eleanor Hills site showed the presence of an endangered species of plant—the *Lyons Pentachaeta*. That species, with small yellow flowers similar to those of the weed oxalis, appears only when the soil is disturbed as with a bulldozer—and had only been added to the state's endangered species list in January. At the time, it was thought to be one of only ten sites on earth where the plant existed but has since been found in a number of other locations. That disclosure immediately required a review, relocation, and reduction in the number of homes planned for the site.

In mid-June the Council approved a $4.1 million budget for the coming '90–'91 fiscal year—$3.2 million for operating expense and $915,000 for capital improvements. It was noted that the previous year had seen $130,000 in legal expenses, due primarily to negotiations involved with the Westlake North Project.

On July 4, the traditional Independence Day parade was held, sponsored and arranged by the Westlake Village Junior Women's Club—walkers, bicyclists, skaters, and baby carriage pilots started as usual from the Westlake Hospital parking lot, and under the watchful eyes of the sheriffs proceeded along Agoura Road and ended at Berniece Bennett Park. Everything that moved was decorated with red, white, and blue, and prizes were awarded. It was a delightful, almost old-fashioned small-town type of celebration greatly enjoyed by participants and observers alike. Fortunately, that parade tradition has continued to delight our citizens.

Celebrating the Fourth of July in Westlake Village. Left to right: David Watson, Sadie Knapp, Jared Knapp, and Summer Knapp. (Courtesy Lussier Photography)

In July, a dispute arose over water meters at the Oak Forest Estates community. Prior to individual ownership of the lots, one water meter served the entire area—with costs paid by the park owner. With the change in ownership and the potential addition of thirty-five new homes, the Las Virgenes Municipal Water District insisted that each home must now have its own water meter—at the homeowner's cost.

On July 26, the City Hall was taken over by the Sheriff's Department and federal agents as headquarters for major drug raids in Agoura Hills. Nineteen arrests were made with individuals from sixteen to twenty-seven years of age booked at City Hall. Marijuana worth an estimated $150,000 was seized in what a sheriff's representative called "open and blatant" activities.

In mid-August the first computer-equipped police cars were deployed in Westlake Village. Use of the $4,000 per car computers was expected to cut down on the occasional delays in response time caused by overly busy radio channels.

The population of the City of Westlake Village had been estimated at 11,300 by authorities, based on a formula of three times the number of registered voters—and some of the city's income from state taxes was based on that figure. Preliminary reports on the U.S. Decennial Census received in late August put the new figure at only 7,402 people residing in 2,928 dwelling units. That figure was much closer to the 1984 estimate of 6,832 by the Southern California Association of Governments (SCAG).

Fourth of July boat parade. (Courtesy Lussier Photography)

Because of a number of complaints, and with the support of the Sheriff's Department, the City Council on September 12 passed an ordinance involving unruly or loud parties. After one visit to the site of the offense, the costs of any subsequent visits to the scene would be billed to the homeowner.

Also in September, the Sheriff's Department became aware of some gang activity at Bennett Park—primarily involving Thousand Oaks gang members who had been chased from their home turf by the Thousand Oaks Sheriff's anti-gang operation. One stabbing had been reported and some graffiti, vandalism, and "doing dope on the school roof" were also logged. On one evening during a meeting at First Neighborhood Community Center two parked cars were "keyed" resulting in major body refinishing, and one of them had both left tires "ice picked" and the driver's window smashed. After brief but intensive activity by the sheriff's deputies Captain Don Mauro was able to state, "Westlake Village does not have a gang problem."

On September 13, the M. J. Brock and Sons application for their Lake Eleanor Hills development was on the agenda for review. However a barrage of new data had been received involving traffic, oak tree removal, and other issues. The Council decided that a supplementary Environmental Impact Report would be required to evaluate such issues, and postponed its decision for at least two months to provide time for more study on the welfare of local butterflies, the Lyons Pentachaeta and traffic.

September also saw some further disaffection at the Oak Forest Estates Community. The State Department of Real Estate was responsible for very long delays in processing the park owners' requests to approve the sale of lots to the tenants. With the allotted time for purchase of lots running out, the vice president of the park's Homeowner Association called for the recall of Bonnie Klove, as one of the Council members in office when the city agreed to the park's conversion. Despite a 6-1 vote of their Board to pursue that recall, cooler heads prevailed and no action was taken.

In mid-October considerable comment was received on the Lake Eleanor Hills proposal. The state attorney general warned the city against taking any action on the issue until botanists could study the area again in the spring when the Lyons Pentachaeta would presumably be in bloom and could be recognized. The Santa Monica Mountains Conservancy, the National Park Service, and the U.S. Fish and Wildlife Service all criticized the Environmental Impact Report because the consultants had not studied the area at the time of year when the endangered species might be in bloom.

The Marriott Hotel company advised in October that they had made a corporate decision to drop their plan for a hotel at Westlake North and was withdrawing their plans for the Residence Inn on Oak Crest Drive.

On November 11 the Council authorized Cotton-Beland Associates to conduct an Environmental Impact Study on the Baldwin Company's proposed project for 394 homes adjacent to the reservoir. The cost was quoted at $122,895.

Mayor Bonnie Klove announced on November 16 that she would not run for a fourth term in the next Council election. In her State of the City address November 25, before an audience of 140 at the Hyatt Westlake, Mayor Klove noted the city's growth, the successful conclusion of the Westlake North negotiations, improvements in public transportation, and the revitalization of The Landing.

Council member Kenneth Rufener was sworn in as mayor for the coming year on December 4, taking over the gavel from Bonnie Klove.

It was noted at the same meeting that December 4 was the deadline for conversion of Oak Forest Mobile Estates property to lot ownership. By that date 133 tenants had opted to buy their lots and twenty-five had qualified for loans from the $1 million low-income fund established by the State Housing and Community Development Department.

On December 12 the Council approved the M. J. Brock and Company Lake Eleanor Hills project for fifty-one homes on seventy-four acres. The approval specified the project would have private roads, and would be separated from Three Springs by an emergency gate at the top of the project. Sidewalks, gutters, or curbs would not be permitted in order to preserve the rural appearance and the developer was to plant additional sagebrush in the area to accommodate more butterflies.

The final action of the year was the signing of an $86,400 contract with Burns-Pacific Construction Company for dredging of the underground portion of the Lindero Canyon Road storm drain. The silt had built up ten feet deep in the tunnel, which is only thirteen feet high, and a "blow out" was feared that could damage parts of the lake marina, as well as grossly contaminate the lake.

1991

After a month's delay caused by arguments from the Baldwin Company, on January 10 the Council approved a $114,495 contract with Cotton-Beland Associates for an Environmental Impact Report for the proposed 393 residences around the reservoir.

Legally, the year started out on a sour note—the state attorney general filed a lawsuit against the city on behalf of the Santa Monica Mountains Conservancy to overturn the city's approval of the M. J. Brock and Sons Lake Eleanor Hills project. The claim was that the city had not received an adequate Environmental Impact Report because there was still danger to the *Lyons Pentachaeta* from the proposed construction of fifty-one homes. The city had reduced the original proposal for ninety homes on the seventy-four-acre site to fifty-one—to allow space for the endangered plant and the butterfly-attracting sagebrush. The developer stated that any further reduction would make the project economically unsound. The lawsuit was ultimately settled when Brock paid the Conservancy $200,000, dedicated thirty acres of land to the Conservancy, and provided a permanent easement across two lots for wildlife access.

On the fifteenth, the Westlake Village Chamber of Commerce contracted with the city for $9,000 to survey all the businesses in the community. Concerns had been expressed that the city might not be getting its fair share of sales taxes (which were 30 percent of the city's total income) due to misapplication of such taxes to another community.

While the city treasurer, Ray Wood, advised the Council that the city was in an excellent financial state, he did note that in the previous fiscal year, '89–'90, while expenses had increased from the prior year by $786,000, the city's income had increased only by $421,000.

In late January the Council approved a $59,000 budget for celebration of the city's tenth anniversary. Tentative plans included concerts in Bennett Park, a presentation of Shakespeare's *Taming of the Shrew* by a local group, a celebratory dinner, and street banners to note the occasion.

In planning for a twenty-five-thousand-square-foot Library on Lot 9 (Oak Crest Drive), the Council retained Deem Lewis McKinley to do a $9,460 preliminary study of parking, site access, soils report, plus a suggested building footprint, placement, and probable costs.

In March, the Council approved a $35,000 contract with the Conejo Recreation and Parks District for a number of tenth anniversary events including *Taming of the Shrew* and a performance of the Conejo Pops Orchestra under the direction of Elmer Ramsey.

The Council hired Municipal Resource Consultants of Westlake Village in March to check on and review the city's sales tax collections. Their fee was 25 percent of any new taxes they found, such as those misapplied to another city because of common zip codes or other reasons.

In April, the Baldwin Company again revised their plan for the development near the reservoir. They eliminated the proposed marinas and any recreational use of the reservoir.

At the first meeting in April, the Council discussed an application for construction of fifty-one condominium units at the former Westlake Stables site on Lindero Canyon Road. The developer, Frank Damavandi of Hollywood, was advised that his plan looked too crowded, and was given two months to develop a new design, based on nine units per acre instead of the twelve as indicated on his plans. It was also suggested that the site might better accommodate commercial uses, rather than residential.

The Council approved a $4,500 grant for "Grad Nite '91," the "Safe and Sober" graduation celebration for Agoura High School seniors. First Neighborhood Homeowners Association gave $500 in support of the event. The total estimated cost was $32,000 to provide the venue, disk jockey, food, decorations, transportation, prizes, lighting, insurance, and security. It was expected that ticket sales would provide about $15,000 toward the expense.

Deem Lewis McKinley presented the study on the proposed Library—with seven options. All required shared parking with nearby companies. The report also noted the possibility of the city purchasing the adjacent Lot 10.

On May 8, the Council voiced strong objections to a plan of the California Transportation Authority (CALTRANS) to install traffic meters on the Lindero Canyon Freeway on ramps. The stated purpose was to control the rate at which cars could enter the freeway—supposedly thus limiting congestion. The Council was aware that opposing the plan might result in CALTRANS refusal to aid financially with the interchange landscaping. (Ultimately, the landscaping was installed—and the ramp meters were not.)

May also saw a major infestation of white flies—a very small insect that caused major damage to pomegranate and other fruit trees. They were also a nuisance to people as they flew in large clouds on the First Neighborhood greenbelts and within yards. Mayor Kenneth Rufener very actively pursued a solution to the problem and convinced county authorities to plant Encarsia wasps in the affected areas—at no cost to the city. Those very small wasps, which did not pose any hazard to humans, were expensive—only one domestic source existed, and most were imported from Israel and Italy. The wasps laid their eggs in the pupae of the white flies, and when they hatched the young wasps would eat their hosts. By end of summer of the first year the white fly population was considerably decreased, and by the second year was wiped out. Then with no food left for their young, the wasps also disappeared.

At the second meeting of the month, the Council reviewed a proposed '91–'92 budget of $3.2 million compared to an expected income of $3.8 million.

In late May, the city signed a contract with Raymond M. Holt and Associates for studies of Library options, possible layouts, and sources of services. The contract for $10,000 was based on completion in ninety days.

Frank Damavandi returned to the Council with a revised plan for condominiums at the stable site—a reduction in density from twelve to ten per acre.

New equipment was purchased in June for the Disaster Response Team and installed at City Hall. The $15,000 investment provided much-needed items—a long-range radio, a TV monitor system for special remote signals to keep city officials informed, and a computer linkage with the Sheriff's Station.

Early in the month, AIL Systems announced the loss of an Air Force contract for manufacture of defensive counter-measure systems used in the B1-B bomber. The result was closure of their Westlake Village facility with the loss of 259 jobs.

On June 14, the Council approved the Damavandi project for fifty-one townhomes on the 4.9 acres below the dam. They were to be built in two- and three-story clusters, with the nine units along Lindero Canyon Road to be held at two stories.

The Wellness Community Valley/ Ventura opened its first office on Lindero Canyon Road in late May, with the first meetings scheduled for early July.

On July 3, the Council agreed to a $30,000 allocation for the Westlake Village Chamber of Commerce, after a presentation by James B. Henderson, the Chamber's vice president for governmental affairs. It was shown that the volume of requests processed by the Chamber was such that if handled by the city would require at least one additional full-time employee.

Raymond Holt, the library consultant, recommended against a joint library with other cities, and noted that it was not possible to get back tax monies paid to the county for library services if the city opted to sign with another agency.

On Sunday, July 14—as part of the city's tenth anniversary festivities—a well-attended concert in Bennett Park featured the singer David Clayton-Thomas.

Political activity started in July when Berniece Bennett took out papers to start her Council re-election campaign, followed shortly by Kenneth Rufener. Jeffrey A. Miller and Daniel Murphy, who also drew papers for his wife, Cynthia, joined Fred Townes and Philip Gatch, the planning director for Thousand Oaks, as candidates. Despite Gatch's stated lack of interest and his view that his candidacy would be inappropriate given his position, Murphy stated, "we have to draft him. . . ."

Dole Food Corporation announced their move from Westwood to two buildings in the Spectrum with a total of 56,000 square feet of space. Also in July,

Concert in Berniece Bennett Park.

a real estate developer in Los Angeles announced plans to acquire the Burroughs site on Lindero Canyon Road–which had been closed for six years. Their plan was to develop a retail center with 375,000 square feet of shops and a movie theater.

At 5 p.m. on Sunday, August 11, as part of the city's tenth anniversary celebration, *The Taming of the Shrew* was presented at Berniece Bennett Park preceded by a family picnic at 3 p.m.

Candidate papers for City Council were filed at City Hall on August 14–by only three candidates: Berniece Bennett, Kenneth Rufener, and Daniel Murphy.

In mid-month, three thousand Encarsia wasps were released to fight the white fly infestation–and the County picked up the tab of one dollar per wasp!

The Westlake Medical Center's general manager, K. D. Justyn, announced plans for a $3 million investment in new high technology equipment and modification. Included in the plans were a Nuclear Spect unit for cardiology, a magnetic resonance imaging unit, and a video endoscopy device. The plans also covered a new admitting office and a cardiac rehabilitation room.

On August 29, given the impossibility of getting any library funds back from the county, the Council opted for an interim solution, to stay with the county and rent five thousand square feet of space for a library.

After a family picnic time starting at 3 p.m. in Bennett Park on September 1, the public was entertained by a musical presentation at 5 p.m. by the Conejo Pops Orchestra under the direction of Elmer Ramsey. The program, attended by almost one thousand people, was another in a series of events noting the city's tenth anniversary.

The Council voted unanimously to pay the $55 per year fee for Westlake Village junior high and high school students using the Thousand Oaks Library for study and reference. Nonstudents were to pay $25 with the city picking up the balance.

In late September, the St. Jude's Catholic School was added to the city's contract with the Sheriff's Department for inclusion in the S.A.N.E. program (Substance Abuse and Narcotics Education). As a stand-alone contract for that service, St. Jude's would have to pay $7,254, but by inclusion in the city's contract they would pay $6,166–a savings to St. Jude's of $1,088.

On September 16, the new Sheriff's Station in Lost Hills was opened for business. Many notables attended both from the county and the five cities served by the station. Sheriff Sherman Block officiated at the formal ceremonies aided by Captain Don Mauro, the captain in charge. The $10 million, thirty-two-thousand-square-foot structure has thirty-two individual cells and a children's playroom.

Dole Food Corporation entered into negotiations in September to purchase the twenty-nine-acre former Burroughs property on which to build its new world headquarters.

In its October 16 edition, *The Acorn* endorsed Kenneth Rufener and Berniece Bennett for reelection to the City Council.

November 5 was Election Day. Berniece Bennett won handily with 1,321 votes, and Kenneth Rufener also won, but by a narrower margin with 1,057 votes to Daniel Murphy's 1,019.

In celebration of its tenth anniversary the city held a dinner at the Hyatt Westlake on November 15. Over 250 attended the occasion, which included a photographic display of the city's progress. Many dignitaries were in attendance, including Cathie Wright representing the state and Elton Galleghy representing the federal government.

At its November 29 meeting, and after Supervisor Edelman had advised the county it could not return library funds, the Council voted to ask the state legislature for an action that would permit the city to pull out of the county system, and to keep the $388,000 currently being paid for that service as part of the property taxes.

On November 25, Mayor Rufener in his State of the City address noted the accomplishments of the year—the

lot sales at the mobile home park, reduced crime and accidents and the defeat of the white fly—"a year of quiet, steady progress. . . ."

The Baldwin Company, still holding an option to build from the failed savings and loans, put their plans "on hold" pending a redesign of the entire project to satisfy some concerns of the Las Virgenes Municipal Water District. The new plan was reported to have eliminated multifamily residences, and to now include thirty-five-hundred- to seven-thousand-square-foot homes to sell in the $750,000 to $1 million range.

77

New Mayor Berniece Bennett, December 4, 1991. (Courtesy Lussier Photography)

On December 4, Berniece Bennett was sworn in as mayor—for the third time—and James E. Emmons was named mayor pro tem.

1992

At the start of the year the Council received requests for $84,000 in community service funding versus $27,000 available for such distribution. In addition there was a sum of $12,000 available for public agencies.

In mid-month City Manager Larry Bagley and lobbyist Kenneth Emanuel visited with State Senator Ed Davis in Sacramento to request his aid in retaining $328,000 a year in taxes if the city opted to use another library service rather than the county's.

Las Virgenes Municipal Water District announced plans to drill wells at several locations, one of them on a First Neighborhood greenbelt within ten feet of a residence. The homeowners, Dr. and Mrs. K. R. Rajagopal, collected hundreds of signatures over one weekend on a petition opposing the action which was soon abandoned by the water district. Permission was granted later for well drilling on city property near Fire Station 144.

Owners of the Westlake Inn Hotel advised in early February they were scaling back their proposed plans for expansion of the property. Council members had voiced objection to replacing the tennis courts with a 40,000-square-foot office and retail center. The proposed addition of 150 rooms was scaled back to 108. In hearings on February 13, the Council continued consideration to March 13, citing concerns about parking at the Inn, and recommended a reduction from 15,500 to 13,000 square feet for the proposed conference center.

Because of the unusually heavy rains, Three Springs residents had expressed some concern about flooding if the reservoir overflowed. Las Virgenes Water District officials gave assurance that there was "no possibility of flooding" of nearby homes, and described the overflow drainage spillway that carried water to a large storm drain at the base of Three Springs Park, from which it would flow to the lake. Concerns had been raised because of problems from flooding in other areas—the destruction of the bridge on Potrero Road, some major flooding in Agoura, a wall collapse along Highway 101 in Calabasas, mudslides in Oak Park, and reports of some flooding in a number of Westlake Village homes.

On March 11, the Council approved plans for expansion of the Westlake Inn—the addition of 108 rooms and a twelve-thousand-square-foot conference and business center. While it was noted that the plan showed a 9 percent deficiency in parking spaces, it was rationalized that not all facilities would be occupied at the same time.

In March the very heavy rains caused the collapse of two three-hundred-year-old oak trees. Their loss was attributed to their large canopy, small root system, and saturated ground.

In March, David H. Murdoch, Board chairman of Dole Food Company, announced the decision to build the world headquarters of the company in Westlake Village. He stated that while locations in Ventura County had been considered, he was "welcomed with open arms" by the City of Westlake Village. He stated that staffing of the new facility would require the hiring of from six hundred to seven hundred more employees.

Late in the month the Baldwin group submitted revised plans for their proposed hillside development adjacent to the reservoir. While they had satisfied some concerns of the Las Virgenes Municipal Water District, some conflict still existed with city ordinances—on ridgeline development, excessive grading, and oak tree removal.

On April 8 the Council approved the purchase of 2 acres on Oak Crest Drive, adjacent to the 1.45 acre Lot 9 already owned by the city. The asking price for the property had been $2 million, but the city was able to close the deal at $1.2 million, partly because of the weakening in interest rates. Financing for the deal was arranged through sale of certificates of participation.

In early May, the Council negotiated a lease for fourteen thousand square feet of space for a City Hall and Library in a building under construction in the Spectrum Business Park. The city

79

Landscape feature at Spectrum Business Park. (Courtesy Lussier Photography)

offered $26–$27 per square foot, but the builder came back with a price $4 to $6 higher. Part of the negotiation was for improvements to be provided by the owner worth $25 per square foot at no cost to the city. Those improvements were expected to cost about $38 per square foot, with the differential of $13 to be paid back by the city over sixteen months. A hitch in the negotiations developed when a limited partner of the builder balked—and insisted the total cost of improvements be limited to $32 per square foot. The lease was finally executed, with the city to pay $24,000 the first month, then $16,000 for the next sixteen months. In mid-June the lease was finally signed for the new City Hall and Library spaces.

Second City Hall.

The Council studied a proposed $4.61 million budget for the upcoming '92–'93 fiscal year, down from the prior year budget of $4.82 million. The reduction was based on expected reduced income from various sources—gas taxes, Proposition A funds, and building fees.

The Baldwin project was again in the news in May when the FDIC asked for a delay in negotiations on the sale of the Westlake Vista property to allow another environmental assessment. The Santa Monica Mountains Conservancy (SMMC), in moving toward their acquisition of the property, claimed they needed more time to search for rare plants on the site. In addition to the *Lyons Pentachaeta* they wanted to search for another rare species. *Dudleya Cymosa Ovatifolia*—one of which it was claimed had been seen from a boat on the reservoir a year before. (The *Dudleya* was not on the state's endangered species list but was being considered as a candidate.)

A letter dated May 25 was sent by Congressman Anthony Beilenson to the FDIC asking for a 120-day delay in its decision on the land sale to Baldwin, following up on the SMMC demand that FDIC honor the policy of giving governmental agencies first option to buy land.

In early June, David Engen applied to the city for a permit to operate a Taco Bell fast food outlet at 32126 Agoura Road, the site of the Coast Savings and

Loan. Many objections were heard—excessive traffic, inadequate parking, a night "hang out" for youths, unsuitability of the location and conflict with the city's image. The project was abandoned when a Coast Savings vice president, in a terse letter, advised they had no intention of vacating the location.

On June 10, the Council approved a five-year lease for the Spectrum Building with two two-year options, with the agreement that it would be ready for occupancy by November. At the same meeting the '92–'93 budget was approved at $4.49 million.

June saw the next chapter in the seemingly never-ending Baldwin project, when the FDIC rejected Congressman Beilenson's request to place a moratorium on the sale to Baldwin.

Amgen, the expanding biotechnology company in Newbury Park announced in June that it was buying two buildings in the Spectrum Business Park for about $3.5 million. The buildings, on the east side of Park Terrace Drive, were to provide 110,000 square feet of space for about two hundred employees.

On June 26 a brush fire threatened twenty homes above Twin Lake Ridge, in one case coming within ten feet of a residence. Fifteen engines, 225 firefighters, four helicopters, three bulldozers, and eight hand crews responded, having the fire under control in five hours.

The Council requested bids on equipment for the new City Hall to permit televising of Council meetings. Three ceiling-mounted cameras, monitors, a control board, and accessory equipment were estimated at $60,000, most of which would be reimbursed by Ventura County Cablevision as part of their franchise agreement.

On July 9, the General Plan Advisory Committee voted 15 to 4 to approve the Baldwin development Westlake Vista of 330 homes on the slopes adjacent to the reservoir.

Two days later, Joseph Edmiston of the SMMC announced that his agency would sue the FDIC unless that federal group would give his state-mandated organization first rights to purchase the Westlake Vista property.

On the twenty-first, the SMMC announced it had voted to offer up to $10 million for the Westlake Vista property.

In late July, an unfortunate incident occurred in First Neighborhood—a home and a car were spray-painted with anti-Semitic slogans and swastikas. Even though the perpetrators were chased by car, they escaped apprehension.

The state had passed a law requiring all cities to reduce their flow of waste to landfills 25 percent by year 1995 and 50 percent by year 2000, with a penalty for noncompliance of $10,000 per day! The city contracted with Emcon Associates at a fee of $70,000 to provide guidance in implementing the requirements. The city hoped for a windfall from the Dole Food Company's dismantling and selling off of the materials from the empty Burroughs/Unisys building. Emcon determined that the flow of waste from the city to the Calabasas landfill was approximately twelve thousand to fourteen thousand tons a year—about 50 percent from residences.

On August 11, a Federal Court judge in Washington, D.C., announced that he would rule shortly on the request by the SMMC to ban the sale of the Westlake Vista property to the Baldwin group. On the thirteenth, U.S. District Court Judge Stanley Harris rejected the request for a preliminary injunction against the sale of the property to Baldwin. At the same time, the FDIC had filed a lis pendens—a warning to potential buyers of pending litigation. Eleven days later Judge Harris vacated the lis pendens.

A fifty-acre brush fire on August 20 came within ten feet of the fence of a Kirsten Lee residence. Over two hundred firefighters from both counties responded, along with four water-dropping helicopters. Aided by thirty-four inmates from Camp Malibu 13, they got a line around the fire at 4:55 p.m. The fire had started near Lake Eleanor about 2:40 p.m. and spread rapidly in the ninety-degree heat.

On August 25, Daniel Keith Ludwig died at age ninety-five at his home in Manhattan. Ludwig, a self-made billionaire and at one time the world's richest man, left most of his fortune to a cancer research organization he had founded in 1971.

Early in September, Jim Johnson noted that recognition of the man who founded the "City in the Country"—Daniel Keith Ludwig—was lacking in the community. He suggested the new Library be named after Ludwig when it was opened later in the year. The Council concurred.

A celebration of First Neighborhood took place on September 19 marking its twenty-fifth anniversary. Roger Wilson, a retired Los Angeles County Sheriff's Department captain noted some families had moved in before all the streets were paved or all the walls were up! Fifteen hundred tickets were sold. Residents of 55 percent of the homes participated, along with over forty families who had moved away, some from as far away as San Francisco. Among those who attended the all-day celebration were some who had grown up in the neighborhood, and then came back with their own children. It was an all-day event—food, music, beer, soft drinks, hot dogs, trick bicycling, a video of the neighborhood development, a full dinner, and then dancing to a large orchestra in the evening that capped a memorable day.

On November 14, the Council approved the M. J. Brock and Sons request for a one-year extension to provide time to prepare and record a final map for the Lake Eleanor Hills housing proposal. The applicant advised of the two-year effort to satisfy the State Fish and Game Department with regard to protections developed to protect the *Lyons Pentachaeta*.

Senate Bill 1816 introduced by State Senator Ed Davis proposed to allow Westlake Village to withdraw from the Los Angeles County Library system and to keep the $345,000 a year of tax money allocated to the library system. The bill was approved almost unanimously by both houses of the legislature but was vetoed by Governor Pete Wilson—leaving the Council members disappointed, perplexed, and upset.

Mayor Berniece Bennett spoke to a large group at the Hyatt Westlake Hotel in her State of the City address on November 20. The new location for the City Hall and the new Library were primary topics, as well as the city's healthy economic condition.

On November 30, the Security Pacific Bank on Agoura Road was robbed at about 2:30 p.m. The perpetrator fled in a vehicle which bank personnel were able to describe in detail. At about 3 p.m. the car was spotted by sheriff's deputies on the 101 Freeway near DeSoto Avenue. A chase followed through city streets to a Van Nuys residential area where the suspect was arrested. Later that day bank personnel identified him.

Richard Nagler, president of The Friends of the Westlake Village Library, presented the city with a check for $50,000 on December 1 for use in furnishing the new Library. Both the Council and the community were most surprised and pleased at the size of the donation.

On December 3, James E. Emmons was sworn in as mayor, and Douglas R. Yarrow became the mayor pro tem. It was noted that Emmons was well qualified to take the gavel since he had so many years of experience as city manager, starting shortly after the city was incorporated.

Early in the month, the Council signed an employment agreement with Raymond B. Taylor to take over as city manager from Larry Bagley who had resigned that post to go into business with his father. Taylor was then the city manager in Malibu, but was seeking a change to a community more like his previous employer, the City of Rolling Hills Estates.

The Baldwin Company made a futile request of the FDIC to provide them with legal assurances—title insurance and other indemnity to protect Baldwin if SMMC prevailed in their suit against FDIC. On December 4, Baldwin then sued FDIC for breach of contract after that agency canceled its plan to sell them the Westlake Vista property, claiming they had spent over three years and $2.5 million in efforts to build the project—$900,000 of which went to the federal government alone. At the same time, SMMCs position was strengthened when the U.S. Department of the Interior proposed placing both the *Lyons Pentachaeta* and the *Dusleya Cymosa Ovatifolia* on the federal list of endangered species.

On December 11, city and Los Angeles County Library officials reached an agreement on a five-year operating contract for the new Library. The program would start with 12,000 items, to be increased to 22,500. The facility would be open forty hours per week with a staff of two librarians, one assistant, and five aides.

On December 30, Haaland Associates, a Thousand Oaks civil engineering firm, was retained by HAS Investment Corporation—now handling marketing for the Resolution Trust Corporation (RTC)—to prepare a Westlake North final tract map that could be submitted for City Council consideration.

In late December, and prior to taking his new post, City Manager-elect Taylor "hit the ground running" by suggesting to the Council that a management audit of all city departments be performed to "assure ourselves that you've got the best level of service at the least cost."

1993

On January 6, Raymond B. Taylor took over as city manager of Westlake Village. His previous posts in that position had included Rolling Hills Estates, a community not unlike Westlake Village.

Early in the month the Federal Deposit Insurance Corporation (FDIC) sent a letter to Congressman Beilenson advising the Westlake Vista property would be offered for sale only to environmental groups for a period of sixty days. This action was taken after the Department of the Interior announced its decision to list the two plant species found on the property as endangered.

On January 13, Concoast Industries, Inc., of Woodland Hills applied to the city for a permit to build forty-five condominium units at the prior Westlake Stables site. The previous applicant, Damavandi Construction, had proposed to build fifty condominiums on that property, but financial problems had developed, the lender foreclosed and resold the property to Concoast. The new application proposed buildings twenty-eight feet high, whereas in the previous proposal they were to be thirty-five feet.

On the seventeenth, the FDIC announced it would be sending preliminary offering circulars to 175 nature and conservancy groups and would offer up to 80 percent financing on the $10 million sale for the Westlake Vista property. The Baldwin Company stated they would continue their lawsuit against the FDIC.

In a February 5 three-hour goals-setting session the Council expressed serious concerns about the state's intent to severely reduce tax returns to cities, and about the state mandates for afford-able housing, even though Mayor

Emmons noted that the city's primary goal was the opening of the new City Hall and Library. The Council's concerns about the affordable housing requirement were based on the state's mandate that Westlake Village provide a total of 160 dwelling units for very low, low and moderate income families—and include means of attaining that goal in the city's General Plan. By definition, annual income levels for a family of four were established by the state as:

Very Low—$19,500

Low—$30,000

Moderate—$45,000

Under State formulas, those families could afford homes priced as follows:

Very Low—$60,000

Low—$91,300

Moderate—$137,500

The Council's quandary—how do we meet the state demands in an almost built-out community with a 1990 median household income of $65,000 (versus $44,000 statewide) and a median price of two-bedroom homes at $212,000?

Dole Food Company, which had moved its headquarters from Westwood to Westlake Village in 1991, announced on February 8 that its 250-employee Packaged Food Division would move from San Francisco to Westlake Village and would occupy part of the recently purchased Spectrum Building. The company's Fresh Foods Division had already moved its 450 employees to a

69,000-square-foot facility at Lindero Canyon Road and Thousand Oaks Boulevard. It was also announced that eventually all groups would be located at the 250,000-square-foot Dole World Headquarters.

City Council members, 1993. Left to right: Berniece Bennett, Kenneth Rufner, Mayor Douglas Yarrow, Kris Carraway, and James Emmons. (Courtesy Lussier Photography)

The Council approved the Concoast proposal to build a forty-three-unit condominium complex on the 4.9-acre site below the dam on February 10, noting that Concoast had cooperated in satisfactorily addressing city concerns on guest parking, driveway access, set-backs, and Lake Management's questions on drainage.

On February 24, City Manager Raymond Taylor advised the Council that Governor Pete Wilson, in announcing an expected state budget shortfall of $7.5 to $8 billion in property tax revenues, also stated that $2.6 billion of those monies earmarked for cities would instead be allocated to the Public Education Fund. Result: the city would receive $150,000 to $200,000 less than expected. The Council then gave consideration to some expenditure reductions. Reduction in sheriff services and postponement of Community Service Fund allocations were discussed for future consideration.

Over the February 23 and 24 weekend, City Hall moved from its original First Neighborhood location to the new headquarters at the Spectrum address—4373 Park Terrace Drive. The city's telephone service had been switched to the new location on the twenty-second and an operator took calls and relayed them as necessary. The staff had been packing for some time in preparation for the move and all were on hand for the task of unpacking in preparation for the opening of business on the twenty-fifth.

Another chapter of the Westlake Vista saga occurred on March 17 when the Santa Monica Mountains Conservancy (SMMC) threatened a lawsuit against the FDIC if that agency refused to consider its bid for the property, even though it was considerably less than the asking price of $10 million.

March 27 was the official dedication date for the new City Hall and Library. The ceremonies started at 11:00 a.m. with the ribbon cutting at noon. Over five hundred attended on a clear, bright day and Lindero Canyon Middle School students presented the flag and sang. Many notables were in attendance— Mayor Emmons introduced Los Angeles County Supervisor Ed Edelman, Sandra Reuben, Los Angeles County Librarian, and State Senator Cathie Wright, each of who congratulated the city on its accomplishments. Tours of the facilities followed the ceremonial ribbon cutting and the new Daniel K. Ludwig Library received kudos from many attending.

It was disclosed in early April that SMMC had offered $5.7 million to the FDIC for the Westlake Vista

property, against an asking price of $10 million. FDIC countered with a reduction in price to $8.1 million. That was not received favorably by the SMMC, whose director, Joseph Edmiston, then stated on the nineteenth that his agency was reinstituting its suit against the FDIC.

County Librarian Sandra Reuben at City Hall and Library grand opening March 27, 1993. (Courtesy Craig T. Matthew)

Daniel K. Ludwig Library grand opening, March 27, 1993.

87

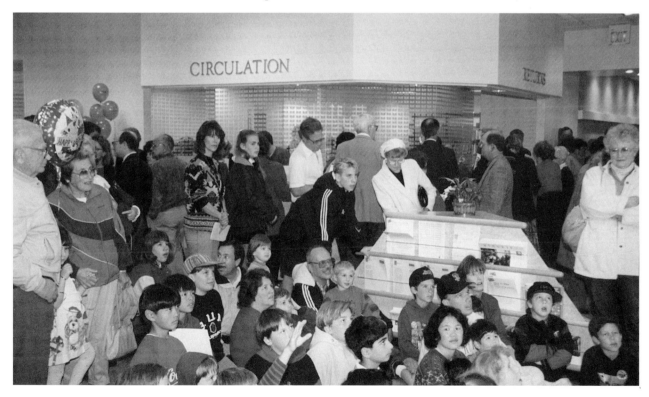

On the twenty-first, the Las Virgenes Municipal Water District (LVMWD) announced plans to bid on the Westlake Vista property and was filing a negative declaration in anticipation of buying the property. It was stated that the LVMWD had no plans for the property but the purchase would allow the land to be kept in its natural state—and there was a possibility of a joint venture with the SMMC.

The Council approved a preliminary plan for Westlake North on May 12. The new plan called for 250 condominiums, thirty-one acres of retail stores, a hotel, and a number of office buildings. It was noted that the new plan was more flexible than previous and could aid the Resolution Trust Corporation in the sale of the property to new developers. Upon approval, the RTC agreed to pay for street and utility engineering work, as well as geological studies. The plan approved differed from the original by combining the thirty-three original lots into fourteen in six specific areas, designated A through F.

Later in May, Jean Lee, a seventy-seven-year-old resident of Westlake Island, was honored by the Council when she was named as the city's honoree for the 1993 Older Americans Recognition Day and she was feted at a later reception by the County of Los Angeles. An accomplished musician, Jean Lee was one of the founders of the Westlake Village Cultural Foundation, which she served well as a director and as president for many years.

The LVMWD general manager announced on June 1 that his agency was negotiating with the SMMC to purchase the Westlake Vista property as a joint venture. The Water District had put a value of slightly over $7 million on the property, with the SMMC expected to contribute $3 million toward the purchase. The acquisition of the property was to be funded by increases in water rates.

By a 3-2 vote on June 9, the Council turned down an ordinance to legalize mobile car washes in the city. That action had been preceded by six months of controversy, much impassioned dialogue from business owners, the arrest of two women washing cars in a parking lot without permission or license, and complaints about the potential contamination of the lake.

On that same date, the Council approved a $3.5 million General Fund budget, which reduced the public safety portion by $244,000 through eliminating one man from the two-man police patrol car.

Westlake Medical Center filed preliminary plans on June 13 for a fifty-four-thousand-square-foot extension to the current structure. A second story and a basement were included in the proposal, which also included a new emergency room, an outpatient surgery unit, and sixty-four more beds, primarily in private rooms.

Early in July, Smith Pipe and Supply Company of Newbury Park moved its operation to larger quarters on Agoura Road in the former Wilkinson Corporation building.

Mid-month saw a lot of action, some of it political—Bonnie Klove announced that she would not run for another term on the City Council noting that she had been on Council since 1981 and had twice served as mayor. Kristine Carraway announced her candidacy for City Council, with the endorsement of Bonnie Klove. James E. Emmons took out papers for re-election to the Council, and Beth Silverman also filed.

On July 14, the Council approved a revised plan for expansion of the Westlake Inn, and the applicant was lauded for the changes proposed. The project called for a new boardroom, improvements in the pool area and sixty-eight new suites—with the first group to include twenty-two executive suites and eight deluxe suites.

In mid-July, less than four months after its opening, the county threatened the Daniel K. Ludwig Library with closure. In a letter to City Manager Raymond Taylor from County Librarian Sandra Reuben, the city was advised the county library system was faced with a loss of $62 million in funding and

there was a possibility of closure of the new Library.

On July 24, Douglas R. Yarrow filed papers to run for a second term on the City Council.

The Council adopted a revised General Plan as required by state law, essentially as drafted by the General Plan Advisory Committee which had been appointed in April of 1991. The action was taken after a lengthy series of public hearings—the most fiercely debated item was the 491 acres around the reservoir. The revised General Plan referred to concerns over water quality, and called for effective management and preservation of the tributary watershed.

On July 28, to the relief of the community, the county adopted a final budget allocating $3.5 million to the library system. That funding permitted the Daniel K. Ludwig Library to remain open, but for only two days each week— if volunteers could be found who would dedicate sufficient hours to assist the reduced county staff.

In August, a thirty-five-year-old mortgage broker, Todd Silver, a graduate of Agoura High School and USC, announced his candidacy for City Council. With one-half hour to go before the August 11 closing hour of 5 p.m. for applications, Daniel J. Murphy filed his papers for a second try at a City Council seat.

On August 11, the county advised the city that sufficient funding would be available to keep the Daniel K. Ludwig Library open four days a week, if a sufficient number of volunteers could be found. The city sent out twenty-one volunteer applications to persons who had expressed interest. Six applications were received with three of the applicants definitely committed to serving the necessary four hours per shift. The Library was then able to stay open four days a week, but only for a total of twenty-eight hours instead of the usual forty hours.

The Westlake Medical Center expansion plans were approved by the Council on September 8. A new cancer clinic was included in a joint venture with Salick Health Care, Dr. Salick's tenth such clinic in the United States. Also included was a twenty-five-thousand-square-foot basement to house a computer-assisted tomography (CAT) unit and radiology equipment. The approval was based on the addition of sixty-seven new parking spaces at the facility.

In mid-September, the Calvary Community Church entered into negotiations with Eaton Corporation to buy their 394,000-square-foot warehouse-type building on La Tienda Drive for $20.5 million. The church had abandoned plans to build a sanctuary on land that it owned in Thousand Oaks near the 101 Freeway after ten years of opposition from neighbors and mounting delays caused by city requirements. Church services had been held for years in a refurbished warehouse-type building on Via Colinas that would hold about one thousand people but with two thousand to accommodate at Sunday services, a new venue was of paramount importance.

Early in October, the SMMC applied to the Los Angeles County Board of Supervisors for an undisclosed amount of Proposition A funding to assist in the purchase of the Westlake Vista property. The Mountains Recreation and Conservancy Agency (MRCA) approved the application since Proposition A funds were intended for parks, beaches, trails, gang prevention, senior and youth services, and acquisition of facilities for public recreation or open space.

The FDIC told the city on October 12 that the sale of Westlake Vista was imminent and that LVMWD had not yet been advised of $400,000 the property owner owed the city for Lindero Canyon Bridge assessments. A fee of $407,890 was agreed upon to cover the balance of the bond, legal fees, administrative costs, and loss of interest, with the city to waive $37,000 in nonpayment penalties that had accrued.

On October 13, the Council passed an ordinance prohibiting smoking in both public and work places. Exceptions to the ban were bars without restaurants, private clubs, and outdoor dining areas.

White Oak Elementary School celebrated its twenty-fifth anniversary on October 15, with events provided by the students, parents, and teachers.

The *Thousand Oaks News-Chronicle* endorsed James Emmons, Douglas Yarrow, and Kristine Carraway for the Westlake Village City Council on October 26 and candidates night was sponsored by the Westlake Village Joint Board of Homeowner Associations on October 28.

Election Day was November 2. With a modest turnout of voters, the final vote tally was:

James Emmons	1,662
Douglas Yarrow	1,542
Kristine Carraway	1,495
Daniel Murphy	771
Todd Silver	705

On November 10, Pierce Brothers received a one-hundred-year permit to operate the Valley Oaks Memorial Park, after promising removal of the crematorium across Thousand Oaks Boulevard from the North Ranch Gateway Shopping Center. The new permit also included the downsizing of the cemetery area from its original 139 acres to the present 40 acres, a change that had been made twenty-five years earlier but had not been included in the county permit, under which the facility had operated prior to cityhood.

At the annual State of the City luncheon on November 19, Mayor James Emmons, recently re-elected to the City Council, noted the city's healthy economic picture. Despite the economic climate which was making it difficult for many cities to balance their budgets, Westlake Village was able to do so without cutting any services. Mayor Emmons also stressed the need for improvement in library services and complimented the community on having already reduced by 25 percent the flow of trash to the landfills.

In late November, the First Neighborhood area finally obtained identification with a new sign in Freedom Square.

On December 1, Douglas Yarrow took over as mayor, with Kenneth Rufener selected as mayor pro tem.

On that same date, the LVMWD announced that escrow was to close in ten days on its purchase of the Westlake Vista property for $6.3 million. Also, LVMWD announced its intention to turn over 477 acres of the property to SMMC when that agency paid half of the sale price. SMMC announced they expected to make that payment by year's end. The escrow actually closed in seven days—on December 8.

The year closed on a high note for White Oak Elementary School when it was selected as a "National Blue Ribbon School" for academic excellence and innovative programs.

1994

In early January the Baldwin Company entered suit against the Santa Monica Mountains Conservancy (SMMC) and the Las Virgenes Municipal Water District (LVMWD) in which they claimed those agencies violated an option agreement that had given the developer first choice to buy the Westlake Vista property. They also claimed to have spent more than $2.5 million in preparing for the construction of 330 homes on the site. The suit also alleged the two agencies had interfered with the longstanding agreement to buy the land that Baldwin had with the Federal Deposit Insurance Corporation (FDIC). Baldwin also sued the FDIC for breach of contract, claiming they had bought a first right of refusal contract from Warmington Homes for $350,000. (Warmington did not own the land, but had paid Vernon Savings for first right of refusal, before that S and L was taken over by the FDIC.)

The disastrous Northridge earthquake occurred on Monday, January 17. That 6.5 Richter Scale temblor caused fifty-seven deaths and many hundreds were injured. Property damage exceeded $4 billion and more than twenty thousand buildings were declared unsafe. Thousands were left homeless when authorities "red-tagged" their residences. Several major aftershocks of 5.0 and 5.5 intensity were felt, adding to the concerns and fright. Las Virgenes schools sustained over $75,000 in damage. Losses in the City of Westlake Village were relatively minor. No injuries were reported but eighteen homes, primarily in First Neighborhood, sustained damage to masonry walls, fireplaces, dry wall, and stucco. Total losses were in the $260,000 range with another $118,000 in damage to commercial structures.

A celebration was held on January 21 on site, to mark the success of the Las Virgenes Municipal Water District in purchasing the Westlake Vista property. Hal Halsey, chairman of LVMWD, spoke of the $6.3 million purchase for the 491 acres from the Federal Deposit Insurance Corporation (FDIC) after protracted negotiations. Jerome C. Daniel, the Santa Monica Mountains Conservancy (SMMC) chair then spoke about his agency's $3.15 million acquisition from LVMWD of 235 acres of the property, plus another 242 acres on the west side of the reservoir. Many others, who had supported the effort to maintain the area as undeveloped open space, also attended the occasion and congratulated the principals on their success.

In February, the County Library's new Online Catalog went into service at the Daniel K. Ludwig Library. It included electronic cataloguing of over six million items in the Los Angeles County Library system, with the information available by author, title, subject, key word, and other search methods. The system responds to requests by advising the location of the requested item and if it is available on loan.

The Thousand Oaks Library sustained major damage from the Northridge earthquake. Steel straps that made up the ceiling structure had collapsed and severely damaged the sprinkler system. Water was released which damaged many books that had fallen from the shelves. To assist in the replacements, Mayor Douglas Yarrow presented a check for $1,000 from the city to Mayor Elois Zeanah of Thousand Oaks.

On March 17, the Council appointed a ten-member panel as the Citizens Advisory Committee to evaluate the city's state of readiness in the event of an emergency and to recommend measures to improve disaster preparedness. (Appendix G)

Many complaints were being received from residents of the Trails in April about the fetid odors emanating from the storm drain channel along Lindero Canyon Road. The south end of the open channel adjacent to the Fire Station was the location where much of the debris collected as it flowed toward the lake not only from First Neighborhood and the Trails but also from areas north of the freeway—Oak Park, Thousand Oaks, and commercial areas. Organic waste products of all types collected in the drain channel—trash, lawn clippings, silt, duck waste—the resulting anaerobic fermentation of which promoted algae growth which in turn generated a sulfide gas. Experts declared the odor was not "hazardous" but agreed it was certainly a "nuisance." Los Angeles County Flood Control had taken responsibility for only the open portion of the channel, and not the underground part that runs from the Fire Station to the lake. Accordingly, they did build net dams near the end of the open portion, which they clean out periodically. A few years earlier the underground part of the channel became clogged with silt, causing "blow-outs" that damaged some docks in the lake. The county denied any responsibility. The city spent over $100,000 to dredge the underground section, as well as about one hundred yards along the lake bottom.

On May 1, Assemblyman Terry Friedman introduced to an Assembly committee a bill, AB2864, which would permit the City of Westlake Village to leave the Los Angeles County Library system—and to keep annual tax funds of $350,000. The bill had the same intent as one introduced earlier by Senator Ed Davis, passed overwhelmingly by both the Assembly and Senate—and vetoed by Governor Pete Wilson. County library officials were opposed to the measure and were instrumental in having SB1448 introduced by Senator David Roberti. That bill was intended to levy a special library tax on local properties. The situation became even more stressful when it was learned that the Daniel K. Ludwig Library was scheduled for closure later in the year by the county—because the city was committed to a five-year lease on the space.

By mid-month, some relief was felt when the county agreed to keep the Library open for three years. The Council then requested the Friedman bill be withdrawn. After the failure of the Roberti bill to gain sufficient support in Sacramento, the Los Angeles County Board of Supervisors voted 3-1 to levy a $30 per parcel tax to help fund a "Community Facilities District" to support Library operations. Sandra Reuben, the county librarian, called it the "one and only option. . . ." The City Council then went on record, 3-2, as not supporting that tax measure.

The traffic situation at the Lindero Canyon and Agoura Roads inter-section was becoming a problem due primarily to vehicles of State Farm Insurance Company employees. The city had previously restriped the street to provide an extra left turn lane on south-bound Lindero Canyon Road for vehicles exiting the freeway. Traffic tie-ups still occurred, making a major problem for other companies in the area, especially at morning rush hour. City officials met with Greg Jones, regional vice president of State Farm. He stated that the Northridge earth-quake had required his company to add about five hundred more claims agents who were temporarily working out of his facility. The company was now operating eighteen vans for the employees. In the discussions, Mr. Jones was asked to study the possibility of staggering arrival and departure times by fifteen minutes to ease the congestion.

After preliminary negotiations with Agoura Hills had failed, in May, Price-Costco announced plans to buy the entire commercial area of Westlake North, with escrow expected to close in June. The owner of record, the U.S. Resolution Trust Corporation (RTC) confirmed the probable sale and Price-Costco announced they were planning to include eight or ten up-scale discount merchandisers—office supplies, sporting goods, etc.—as well as a number of fast food operations at the site.

The RTC, which owned 90 percent of Westlake North, bought the other 10 percent from Home Savings Association to bring their ownership to full holding for the sale to Price-Costco. It was disclosed that Price Company (prior to the merger with Costco) had started negotiations with the RTC in the fall of 1993.

On July 11, the Council agreed to name the new loop road that was to go through Westlake North "Russell Ranch Road" in honor of the family that had owned and operated the ranch on the property for generations. Patricia Russell Miller who had been raised and lived on the ranch even after it was sold, when told of the honor, is reported to have said "Sounds good, I think that's nice."

On the thirteenth, the Council approved a contract with Cotton-Beland Associates for another EIR on the Westlake North property, required because the RTC had made changes to the basic plan for the site.

J. M. Peters Company had built thirty-three large homes on some of the land to the east of the Fire Station. In late July the Warmington Homes Company proposed a plan to the city to build seventeen somewhat smaller homes on the rest of that property. Both the Westlake Trails Association and some homeowners in the J. M. Peters homes objected to their size, "tract" appearance and considerably lower cost.

Warmington revised the plans to make the homes somewhat larger and more individually distinctive, which raised their prices—and ultimately obtained the approval of both the city and the Trails.

In late July, an attempt was made by the Las Virgenes Unified School District to build a parking lot on a strip of ground directly across the wall from homes on Crownfield Court. After protests by nearby residents, agreements were reached to provide street parking permits for teachers on Village School Road and more importantly, to turn over landscaping responsibilities on the strip adjacent to the homes to the First Neighborhood Property Owners Association. As the lawn and irrigation was being upgraded, neighbors Nancy and Jack Bannon donated five good-sized trees—three jacarandas and two crepe myrtles—which were planted at a ceremony attended by the superintendent of education.

In August, the Environmental Protection Agency, the EPA, issued strong warnings to all cities on storm water run-off, which could contaminate rivers and oceans. Unless actions were taken to educate the public about run-off problems and to cite offenders, cities would be subject to a fine of up to $25,000 a day! A program was instituted by the National Pollution Discharge Education System (NPDES) to require cities to reduce pollution "to the maximum extent practicable." In response, the city provided stencils and paint and all catch basins in the city were marked by volunteer groups, including the Rotary Club, the Chamber of Commerce, Westlake Medical Center, and St. Jude's, with the words, "Don't Dump—Drains to Lake."

On August 10, over two hundred people attended Disaster Preparedness night presented by the Agoura Hills team at the First Neighborhood Community Center. It was announced that classes in Disaster Preparedness for Westlake Village residents would start on August 22 in Agoura Hills.

On September 5, the Council received a formal application from Price-Costco for approval of plans for a 127,000-square-foot Price-Costco store, plus another 155,000 square feet for five anchor stores, other shops, and fast-food stores.

The Council approved Warmington Homes' revised plans for more diverse home designs, which would be priced in the $500,000-and-up range. The Trails Association also found the redesigns acceptable.

On the twenty-eighth, the Council gave approval to a $5.5 million expansion plan for the Westlake Inn, including a thousand-square-foot Presidential Suite plus thirty-eight other suites.

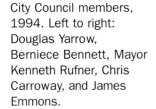

City Council members, 1994. Left to right: Douglas Yarrow, Berniece Bennett, Mayor Kenneth Rufner, Chris Carroway, and James Emmons.

In late September, Western Pacific Homes of Irvine proposed 239 single-family homes in the $150,000 price range to be built in the twenty-seven-acre residential section of Westlake North. They advised they were in negotiations with the RTC to purchase the land for the two- and three-bedroom homes of eleven hundred to fifteen hundred square feet.

In October, some homeowners in Agoura Hills' Lake Lindero development expressed concerns and anger about contamination to their thirteen-acre lake. They were convinced this would occur because of the Westlake North development. City officials tried to calm their concerns by pointing out that plans for drainage, hydraulics, grading, and storm sewers all had built-in protection designed specifically to negate any possible contamination of Lake Lindero. In addition, it was noted that silting basins would be required during construction phases to further insure against any such contamination to their lake.

At a celebration in Washington, D.C., White Oak Elementary School was again honored with the National Blue Ribbon Award for excellence and innovation. Principal Richard Malfatti and Board President Amy Berns attended the ceremonies and were pleased when Vice President Al Gore singled out White Oak for special mention.

On November 1, the Council received a letter from the City of Agoura Hills objecting to the Price-Costco store, asking for another EIR and stating, incorrectly, that large stores of that type were not being considered when the 1989 plan was approved. The letter also expressed concerns about outside traffic that would be generated within their city.

About thirty-five Westlake Village volunteers completed basic training on Disaster Preparedness in Agoura Hills prior to the establishment of the Westlake Village team on November 2.

In mid-November, planning officials in Thousand Oaks and Agoura Hills stated that their cities should not be required to pay for any improvements that might be required by developments at Westlake North.

At about that same time, a traffic study of twenty-six locations showed that the Westlake North development would have impact at only four inter-sections—three of them within the city. The fourth location, a left turn at Thousand Oaks Boulevard and Kanan Road in Agoura Hills, had already been tagged as a problem site.

Good news developed in mid-November: the county increased the time the Library would be open from twenty-eight hours a week to forty-five hours.

Early in December, a group started to organize in opposition to the Price-Costco store. About eighty-five people attended a meeting to hear all the objections: primarily traffic and impact on small businesses. An informal petition survey was taken and some signatures were obtained.

On December 8, the hospital conglomerate Columbia HCA announced the acquisition of Westlake Medical Center from Universal Health Services, in an exchange of facilities.

After the Northridge earthquake in January, concerns had been expressed about the safety of the Westlake Reservoir dam. The Las Virgenes Municipal Water District stated the dam's integrity was unbreached, as shown by the measurements taken twice a year at twenty-eight locations with brass caps embedded in concrete monuments.

Near the end of the year, Windstar Homes, Inc., of Orange County app-roached the city with a concept for affordable senior housing to be located southeast of the Ridgeford Drive–Lindero Canyon Road intersection. The property, currently owned by Cedars-Sinai Hospital, was proposed for up to 149 units of four hundred to five hundred square feet, located in three-story buildings.

1995

By early January, winter rain storms started to take their toll. The lake was filled to overflowing, cresting the dam by almost four feet. Docks floated away as the high waters raised them from their moorings. The Lake Management crews were busy trying to salvage boats that had come adrift before they reached the dam. Tons of silt and debris were washed into the lake from Potrero Creek. The velocity and volume of the water from the creek undermined a wing wall at the Triunfo Canyon Bridge and endangered a nearby residence. After the rains and the high water subsided, some boats were found well up on dry ground. Several homes in Three Springs were flooded and the Three Springs Park was inundated as well. Previously unknown springs appeared and added their flows to the rising waters.

In order to allow the use of radar in attempts to curb speeding, the Council found it necessary to raise speed limits on the five main streets in the city. That action was taken in a 4–1 vote to comply with the state-mandated ruling that permitted the use of radar only if the posted limits were at least 85 percent of the actual speed at which motorists drive on a particular street.

In February, the city manager reported that halfway through the fiscal year the city was in good financial condition—at only 42 percent of budget. Receivables were at 47 percent including one-half million dollars received from the Dole Food Company. A $150,000 budget adjustment was requested to permit early street repairs, an item that had been deferred but was now needed because of damage caused by the heavy rains.

In mid-March, the Westlake Village Rotary Club presented its second Street Fair. It was surprisingly successful. The city permitted Lakeview Canyon Road to be blocked off between Agoura Road and Watergate and over one hundred merchants set up their stands in the street, selling food, curios, clothing, and gift items. The Westlake High School Chorus and Scottish and Irish dancers entertained the crowds throughout the day. Children were pleased to sit in a fire engine from nearby Station 144. Westlake Medical Center had a tent in their driveway where free blood pressure testing was available. The success of the venture and its acceptance by the public insured it would be repeated annually.

In mid-April, the first group opposed to the approval by the City Council of a Price-Costco store held a meeting at the Westlake Village Inn. Just thirty-seven people attended, many of them from Agoura Hills and Oak Park, and discussed a recall of four members of the Council if they voted for the store. One city resident called for a lawsuit against the Council for possible violation of the Environmental Protection Act, noting that the cost of such legal action would be in the range of $50,000 to $100,000. At about the same time, another anti–Price-Costco group organization calling themselves "Citizens for Westlake" met to discuss strategy.

For the first time, the Council reviewed a two-year budget in May. It was noted that a '95–'96 General Fund budget of $4.05 million represented a 6 percent decrease from the prior year due to general economic conditions. One example cited was the decrease in sales tax revenues from $157 per capita in 1991 to $128 per capita in 1994.

After having been named Conejo Valley Woman of the Year in 1983, Dorothy L. Brockway was honored by the city on May 12 for her many services to the community for the past twenty-five years. As the city's nominee at the Older Americans Recognition Day event sponsored by the County of Los Angeles, she was presented with a scroll from the county supervisors at a downtown luncheon and was then presented with a certificate of recognition in a brief ceremony at City Hall.

The Council allocated $20,000 to the Westlake Village Chamber of Commerce in June in continuance of an agreement to provide services to the community, for activity in economic development and for providing city information to residents and to outside interests.

The Council also took action in June to set November 7 for the next City Council election.

After eighteen months of effort and intensive training, the city's new Disaster Response Team reported to the City Council in July that it has reached its three primary goals. First was the preparation of a Disaster Preparedness booklet and its distribution to all households and businesses in the city. Secondly, the by-laws and constitution for the Team had been completed and approved by the Council. Third, all members of the Team had completed at least twelve hours of intensive training in all aspects of disaster response.

In early July, Berniece Bennett, a fourteen-year Council member and three-time mayor, announced that she would not be running again for a Council seat in the upcoming election.

With the lessening in property values, the Los Angeles County Fire Department was facing a significant shortfall in revenues from the property tax base, which would affect the level of services they were able to provide. Representatives of the Department were visiting cities to ask for support in their efforts to have property taxes increased by $20 per year so they could continue

the same level of fire protection and paramedic services. On July 26, the Council voted to support the Department's efforts.

On that same date, Dakota-Smith, a producer of designer eyewear, was advised by the Council that they must submit detailed plans for all the external decorative features they desired to incorporate on and around their new building in the Spectrum Business Park. Dakota-Smith officials advised they hoped to break ground in August and were targeting February as the move-in time for their sixty employees.

In early August, Westlake Medical Center announced the closure of its obstetrics unit and the transfer of all maternity services to Los Robles Hospital. Ronald Phelps, the president and C.E.O. of Los Robles announced that the Westlake facility would get an eighteen-bed rehabilitation unit for patients requiring extended care. It was noted that at the time of the acquisition of the Westlake facility by Columbia HCA, the Council had written Columbia urging retention of the Westlake emergency room and trauma service.

In August, the Price-Costco issue heated up, with a recall notice being sent to Councilwoman Kris Carraway on the fifteenth and another to Councilman Douglas Yarrow on the nineteenth. The notices accused them of failure to follow the will of the people and had been issued by a group calling themselves "Westlake Residents Opposed to Non-Responsive Government"or"WRONG." Still another group was organized to oppose Price-Costco, calling themselves "United Communities Against Price-Costco" and claiming to represent residents of Agoura Hills as well as Westlake Village. The 1989 agreement specifically allowed a 120,000-square-foot store on the Westlake North property. Abrogation of that agreement could nullify the two-hundred-year open space easement the city received on the golf course. Furthermore, it could cost the city up to $3 million in penalties. The groups continued their attempts to block Council action. On the twenty-fourth, Superior Court Judge Robert H. O'Brien ruled that the Council had not erred on its approval and the Price-Costco development should continue. That did not deter the opponents and WRONG proceeded with the recall action, which would require 1,274 favorable votes to succeed.

Council members Carraway and Yarrow organized to fight back against the recall action, citing Judge O'Brien's decision and the many expressions of support from city residents. Those sentiments were expressed by donations to the anti-recall movement of $5,000

in just eighteen days. On September 5, the *Los Angeles Daily News* called the recall action both "frivolous" and "misguided." On September 7, the city clerk returned the anti-Carraway petition as incomplete—state law allows a statement from the recall target to be included in the recall petition and Carraway's full statement was not included. One of the recall leaders stated that part of Carraway's statement was wrong in that it alleged he had stated that the majority of Price-Costco opponents would support a special tax to fund a breach of contract liability. However, a recording of a radio interview disclosed that he had said, "assess each homeowner $500, $600—whatever it is, we have X house-holds. We can certainly assess $3 million." That same recall advocate was quoted as opposing Council candidates Betty DeSantis and James Henderson because they were pro-City Council and urged support for candidates David Woodruff and Steve Hessick because they were anti-Price-Costco (both of whom distanced them-selves from his actions prior to the election).

On September 18, the Council approved the wording of the petition, with Carraway's statement intact and the petitioners were the able to start their campaign to get 25 percent of the city's 5,105 registered voters to sign.

Election Day was November 7, with final vote counts of:

DeSantis	1,051
Henderson	899
Woodruff	499
Hessick	405
Stein	374

On November 15, the chief attorney for the University of Southern California warned the "WRONG" group to stop using the USC name and threatened legal action. "WRONG" had claimed that a "USC study" stated a Price-Costco would result in reduced property values in the area—the statement had apparently been extracted from a letter written by a USC professor.

Kenneth Rufener, the outgoing mayor, presented the annual State of the City address at a Hyatt Westlake luncheon on November 16. He enumerated the many city achievements during the year—among them the approval of Price-Costco after months of dissension, the Dole Food Company decision to build its world headquarters in the city, and the start of two new housing tracts.

In late November, a petition was circulated at Hughes Market on Thousand Oaks Boulevard opposing Price-Costco. Of the 120 signatures obtained less than 25 percent were from Westlake Village residents.

Supervisor Zev Yaroslavsky of Los Angeles County and Supervisor Frank Schillo of Ventura County were the guest speakers at a breakfast in the

City Council members, December 6, 1995. Left to right: Douglas Yarrow, Kris Carraway, Mayor James Emmons, Betty DeSantis, and James Henderson.

Hyatt Westlake Hotel on December 1. At the event, sponsored by the city and the Westlake Village Chamber, both speakers addressed their county budgets as well as the subject of economic development.

December 6 was the first live telecast of a City Council meeting. Betty DeSantis and James Henderson were sworn in as new Council members by Judge Lawrence Mira, followed by the swearing in of James E. Emmons as mayor and Douglas R. Yarrow as mayor pro tem. Many plaques, citations, and awards were presented to outgoing Councilwoman Berniece Bennett and Mayor Kenneth E. Rufener, both of whom had announced their retirement from public office.

The City of Agoura Hills Planning Commission voted 3-1 in mid-December to approve a driving range at the Lake Lindero Country Club. The twenty-four-tee facility was to be night-lighted until 10 p.m. It was noted that the tees were 115 feet from homes on Cape Horn Drive in Agoura Hills and only 105 feet from homes on Logwood Drive in Westlake Village. Numerous protests were registered, particularly from the nearby Agoura Hills residents but assurances were given that the facility would not become a nuisance. The proposed range property included part of the Southern California Edison easement within Westlake Village city

limits, which the commissioners and the club stated they were entitled to use. Since its construction, despite efforts to modify it and many complaints from both residents and the City of Westlake Village, the night lighting and errant golf balls have posed a continuing problem for residents along Logwood Drive.

1996

In early January, Western Pacific Housing submitted plans to the city for construction of 183 single-family detached homes on the twenty-eight acres of Area F in Westlake North. The area had been originally planned for 250 attached condominium units. Council members had visited a site in Orange County to evaluate a very similar development of homes ranging from 1,060 to 1,750 square feet. On that visit it was noted that driveways were too short to accommodate parked cars, but the developer advised the proposed homes would have longer driveways suitable for parking.

On January 3, Columbia HCA announced plans to discontinue in-patient care services at Westlake Medical Center, citing a patient occupancy of only 11 percent of capacity and a loss of $1 million over the preceding six months. It was also announced that some of the employees would be transferred to Los Robles Hospital. At the same time, Dr. Bernard Salick who was leasing about one-quarter of the hospital for his Comprehensive Cancer Care Center, reiterated his commitment to purchase the facility and noting his doubts that any space would be available for any Columbia services. Dr. Salick also stated the sale would be finalized within ninety days but no other information would be available, citing a confidentiality agreement.

In mid-month the Council received a report from the sheriff advising of a material increase in serious crimes in the city, from 188 in 1994 to 288 in 1995—a jump of 53 percent. Vehicle burglaries of cell phones and other valuables led with 87 incidents. At about the same time, the Sheriff's Department advised of the apprehension of a group, which had been burglarizing vehicles in church parking lots during Sunday services. Suspects had been spotted in a Calvary Community Church parking lot, then followed to St. Jude's where they were apprehended and some stolen items were recovered.

In mid-February, the "WRONG" group, which had opposed the Price-Costco approval, was again in the news, this time for failing to file a financial report by January 31 with the state. The law requires that all income and expenditures of political candidates or committees be filed by that date. One of the "WRONG" leaders stated the

report would be filed by February 16 and estimated the group's income approximated $5,000 from eighteen contributors. The report had still not been filed at the end of the month. The opposing group supporting the two Council members had filed a timely report, citing income of $5,978 and expenses of $2,071.

At the February 14 Council meeting, Price-Costco announced that construction was proceeding on schedule and a target date for opening was June 4. It was also noted that ten temporary drainage and settling basins had been completed to trap sediment and control erosion until the large storm drain piping could be completed.

The next chapter in the Westlake Vista saga involved a federal court action awarding Baldwin $8.7 million plus $2.5 million in lost profits, to be paid by the Las Virgenes Municipal Water District (LVMWD) and the Santa Monica Mountains Conservancy (SMMC). The agencies viewed the verdict as a victory of sorts because Baldwin had sued for over $42 million. In a prior action, Baldwin had also sued the Federal Deposit Insurance Corporation (FDIC) for $7 million. In the settlement, Judge Madeleine Flier ruled that the two agencies had "conspired to wrongfully interfere" with the Baldwin-FDIC deal, and that the $8.7 million should be divided, with FDIC paying $7 million and the two local agencies paying the $1.7 million.

After hearing from a number of citizens that they had not been adequately informed on the Price-Costco matter, the two new Council members Betty DeSantis and James Henderson were assigned to an ad hoc committee to explore ways to keep the public better informed. The recommendations, presented at the March 13 Council meeting, included a monthly newsletter covering all major city activities, to be sent to all households, more press releases by staff and quarterly meetings with representatives from each of the city's homeowner associations.

During the month of March, the "WRONG" group finally filed its financial statement as required by state law. Instead of the estimated $5,000 claimed as income, the actual figure reported was $908, $350 of which had come from three individuals. Expenses of $1,500 were reported, with one of the principals paying the difference.

A resident of the city, William J. McSweeney, was appointed captain in charge of the Lost Hills Sheriff Station by Sheriff Sherman Block.

In early April, Superior Court Judge Flier reduced the jury award of $7 million to Baldwin, classifying it as "double recovery."

On April 10, the Council approved solicitation of bids for refurbishment at both Three Springs Park and Berniece Bennett Park. Included in the plan for the latter was the removal of the Tot Lot from under a large oak tree, because of concerns raised when another large and mature oak in the area had fallen, fortunately with no personal injuries. It was noted that not only would new Tot Lots have to be built to Americans with Disabilities Act (ADA) standards but that a shade cover would also be required to provide protection from the sun once the facility was moved from the shade of the oak tree. Total cost for the two parks was estimated at $180,000.

At the meeting on April 24, the Council agreed to request inclusion in the upcoming November election an initiative intended to provide funds for parks and instructed the city manager to prepare and submit an application and supporting data to the agency, "Trust for Public Land." The request for $1.3 million was to cover the acquisition of Lot 79 on Lindero Canyon Road, the necessary earth moving and the construction of two baseball fields and two soccer fields with appurtenant structures.

On May 2, 283 full- and part-time employees of Westlake Medical Center were given the legally required sixty days notice of the hospital's closure planned for June 30. On that same date the Los Angeles County Fire Department assigned a second paramedic unit to Station 65 at Cornell and Kanan Roads.

The Western Pacific housing construction project was finally approved on May 8, but by only a 2 to 1 vote, after reduction in number of homes to 179 and an agreement to build a Tot Lot. (One absence and one abstention accounted for the vote count.)

In mid-month the city manager presented the budget proposal for fiscal year '95-'97 showing an expected surplus of $2.5 million, due largely to a final payment of $2.9 million from Westlake North due in May 1997. Included in the recommendations was a substantial increase in service hours by the Sheriff's Department.

On May 29, the city received disappointing news from the "Trust for Public Land." Even though the proposal presented to them by the city was considered excellent and well qualified for a grant, it could not be considered. Under their guidelines, even one letter of objection to a proposal would disqualify it from consideration. They had received that one letter—from a Westlake Canyon Oaks resident.

On May 26, Columbia HCA announced it would continue to operate an urgent care facility at Westlake Medical Center after it was closed, if an agreement could be reached with Dr. Salick on leasing space after he took possession of the facility.

The Council took initial action on June 4 to rezone the entire former Westlake Vista property from residential to open space. The purpose was to forestall a proposed swap by the SMMC of the lower 80 acres of the property with the Baldwin Company, in exchange for 150 acres in Calabasas that SMMC wanted to acquire.

In June, *Worth Magazine* rated the City of Westlake Village among the three hundred wealthiest communities in the country—with an average household annual income of $109,500 and an average home value of $432,500.

Dole Food Company presented plans for its world headquarters on the property at Lindero Canyon Road and Via Colinas. The three-story, 527,000-square-foot building was estimated at a cost of $35 million. Construction was scheduled for completion in 1998.

Plans were announced for construction of shops at Westlake North—a fifty-thousand-square-foot Albertson's, a twenty-six-thousand-square-foot Petsmart, and a twenty-four-thousand-square-foot Staples. It was also announced that the new opening date for Price-Costco would be August 9.

In mid-June the Council by a vote of 4-1 approved a four-hundred-square-foot outside dining area for the Oishii Restaurant, although the parking problem had not yet been resolved.

As previously announced, the Westlake Medical Center and its Emergency Room were closed on July 1. The entire facility reopened on July 3 as the Comprehensive Cancer Center under Dr. Salick. A Los Angeles Superior Court judge had issued an order on July 3 for the hospital to stay open until July 18, but not only was the hospital already closed, its license to operate had expired. On July 4 the *Los Angeles Times* quoted Dr. Salick as responding to a press interview question, "We do not operate emergency rooms."

The Council was faced with a question in July regarding the Transient Occupancy Tax (TOT). Should action be taken by the Council to increase the tax from 6 percent to 10 percent (as had been done in neighboring cities) or should the matter be put on the ballot for the voters to decide—as required by Proposition 62 passed earlier this year? However, Proposition 62 had been legally challenged and was tied up in the courts where appeals were expected to take years. The Council decided to apply the 4 percent tax increase and then wait for some final clarification by the courts or the state legislature.

The Council took action in July to extend for two years the tentative tract

107

Entrance to Westlake North Shopping Center showing the monument sign. (Courtesy Lussier Photography)

map for the development then known as Lake Eleanor Hills. The original developer, M. J. Brock and Sons, had abandoned its interest in the development due to the downturn in housing sales. The SMMC had sued the city claiming the 1990 Environmental Impact Report was inadequate, and Brock had agreed to pay $200,000 to SMMC for "offsite mitigation" (protection for *Lyons Pentachaeta* and the indigenous butterflies).

A proposal was received from Richland Westlake for a modification to the Westlake North Specific Plan, which would allow an elementary school and playground to be built adjacent to the Freeway. LVUSD favored the proposal, but many doubts were expressed about the planned location.

Costco main entrance, August 1996.

After several months of review and argument, Oishii Restaurant was declared to be in code compliance and was permitted to increase its outdoor dining area from 400 to 1,060 square feet.

On July 19, a Superior Court judge ordered the sale of Westlake Medical Center. Salick purchased it with restrictions on the type of services he could provide—cancer, dialysis, organ transplants, and immune deficiencies. Columbia HCA had asked that the restrictions "run with the property" to prevent Salick from reselling the facility to a third party for operation as a full-service hospital. Escrow then closed on the property at midnight on July 24, at the agreed price of $8.15 million. The turnover was less than friendly, with accusations and threats of lawsuits against individuals.

On July 24, the Council approved a General Plan amendment as the final action in rezoning the 481 acres known as Westlake Vista from residential to open space.

The Costco store opened on schedule August 9 with an estimated attendance of over three thousand. A free breakfast was served to many of the first-day attendees and the store was packed with people from the time it opened that day. Many admired the outside appearance of the structure, with its off-white stucco, arches, tile facings, and landscaped planters.

On August 20, Dr. Salick amended his lawsuit against Columbia HCA alleging attempts to stifle competition. He claimed they restricted services he could provide. He also alleged they attempted to harm him by spreading rumors by influencing his British partners, Zaneca, Ltd., during sale negotiations.

Santa Rosa Homes of Orange County had proposed building a seventy-five-unit senior housing project on the 4.4-acre parcel across Triunfo Creek from Oak Forest Mobile Home Estates. On September 25, the Council upheld a ban on such construction previously imposed by Los Angeles County, citing flooding concerns, negative environmental impacts, traffic, and access problems.

At about 5 a.m. on September 26, a major fire broke out at The Sound of Billiards in the North Ranch Gateway Shopping Plaza. The explosive nature of the fire blew window glass and blinds out onto Thousand Oaks Boulevard and broke several heavy roof beams. Twenty firefighters had it extinguished in about a half-hour, then spent most of the morning securing the site. The Westlake Village Chamber of Commerce offices, which shared the building with the billiards parlor suffered both smoke and water damage to their records and equipment, despite efforts by the fire-fighters to protect them with tarpaulins. An investigation of the fire was immediately started when containers of gasoline

were found at the site. Damage to the building was such that it had to be about 90 percent rebuilt.

The hospital was again in the news in late September when the name was changed to Salick Specialty Hospital. A proposal was made to add a radiation unit in an eleven-thousand-square-foot addition, and the CEO of Los Robles Hospital for the first time disclosed an offer to amend the purchase agreement so Salick could operate an emergency room. Dr. Salick confirmed that the offer had been made and refused.

October 6 saw a celebration in Bennett Park marking the city's fifteenth anniversary. The event coincided with the opening of the new Tot Lot with its up-to-date play equipment and flexible rubber flooring under the sand. Free food was available. The Agoura High School Band entertained the crowd, as did the local band "Playback." A major

Fifteenth anniversary logo by student Julianne Peckinpah.

feature at the celebration was the sale of T-shirts imprinted with a drawing of mountains, a lake with boats, and the sun, with the slogan "Happiness is growing up in Westlake Village" as designed by a White Oak Elementary student, Julianne Peckinpah.

Late in the month the Council held protracted discussions on potential locations for a new City Hall and Library. With the current lease on the present

quarters due to expire in January of 1998, and even though a two-year extension could be negotiated, it was deemed essential that decisions be made on "rent or buy or build." A number of locations were considered and it was agreed that the Foxfield site should be dropped from consideration. It was also agreed that consideration should be given to building on the city-owned Lots 9 and 10 on Oak Crest Drive or to purchase an office building in First Neighborhood which was for sale at a price of about $900,000. Discussions were also held on whether the two facilities—the Library and the City Hall—should be separate or together in one structure.

For the first time, the newly trained Disaster Response Team was out in force on Halloween night to assist Sheriff's deputies in case any disturbances occurred. The team kept in touch by shortwave radio, with their communications hub located in Three Springs Park.

Early in November, the two-screen Westlake Village Movie Theater closed-- leaving a sign on the marquee "Closed permanently. Thank You For Your Patronage." In a newspaper interview, the proprietors stated they could no longer compete with the large, first-run multiscreen theaters in the area.

On November 6, after four hours of conflicting testimony on changes to the Westlake North Specific Plan proposed

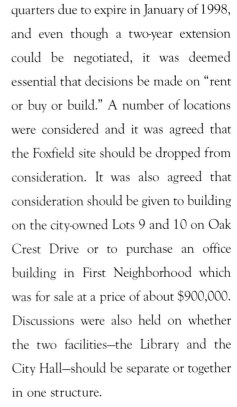

Mayor James Emmons announces retirement, November 21, 1996. (Courtesy Lussier Photography)

110

by Richland Westlake, the Council held off on making a decision. The changes included 259 more single-family homes in the area south of the Renaissance housing tract. This area was zoned for office structures and a promised donation of 11.2 acres to be used for an elementary school and park. At a subsequent meeting on the thirteenth, the Council rejected Richland's proposal by a 3–2 vote—to the disappointment of the School District.

At the State of the City luncheon held at the Hyatt Westlake Plaza on November 21, Mayor James E. Emmons announced that having served two terms on Council, he would not be running for re-election.

On December 4, Douglas R. Yarrow was sworn in as mayor for the coming year, and Kenneth E. Rufener was named mayor pro tem.

1997

At the beginning of the year, the city's forty-member Disaster Response Team advised the City Council of additional items required to provide adequate services to city residents in the event of an incident that would cut the community off from even a short period of outside help or communication. Short-wave radios, generators and electrical cables, lighting fixtures, medical supplies, and other items were listed. The cost was estimated at $35,000

against the Team's $5,000 budget. The Council agreed to increase funding by $15,000 for the current fiscal year, with a like sum to be allocated in the next fiscal period.

In early January, the PYJ Corporation, operators of the Westlake Village Golf Course, proposed to build seventy-foot-high screens around the entire course. After objections to the height, a compromise was proposed that would keep the screens at seventy feet along the freeway but reduce them to forty-five feet along Agoura Road. Objections to that proposal were voiced on the basis that it would hurt the visual quality of the community. The applicant did not have available any specifics on damage or injuries caused by errant balls and was asked to return with the specific data verifying the number of claims against them and what impact the screens were expected to have on their insurance rates.

The Landing, the one-hundred-thousand-square-foot business and restaurant complex on the lake came under new management when its Japanese owners, in liquidating their assets, sold the complex to Dolphinshire Partners for $11.7 million. The new owners announced a five-year plan to fix up the parking lot, renew the landscaping, and paint all five buildings.

In late January, it was disclosed that Tenet Healthcare Corporation of

Santa Barbara was considering the establishment of an urgent care facility in Westlake Village. The site under consideration, near the intersection of Westlake Boulevard and Hampshire Road, also housed the Westlake Breast Center.

At its February 12 meeting, the Council started discussions and studies on proposed locations for a new City Hall and Library. At the following meeting on the twenty-sixth, the Council voted 3-2 to obtain more information about all possible locations for the site, including city-owned property on Oak Crest Drive, the First Neighborhood office building, and—back in contention—the Foxfield site.

In late February, the Council opted to join other cities in opposing Proposition 62—the proposal to require cities to put any new taxes to a vote of the electorate. The Howard Jarvis Taxpayers Association was suing the City of La Habra and Westlake Village wanted its name included in a "Friend of the Court" brief to be filed in March. That Westlake Village action was part of a concerted drive by the League of California Cities to allow cities to keep tax funds previously collected without voter approval.

On March 7, to the pleasure of many residents, the Westlake Village Movie Theater reopened as the Regent Westlake. The new owners, Mark R. Harris and Paul Colichman, had refurbished the facility with new seats and carpeting and announced they would be showing art, foreign, and specialty films. Theater One opened with a choice from the "Best Art Films of 1996," *Il Postino*.

On Sunday, March 16, the Westlake Village Rotary Club held its third annual Street Fair on Lakeview Canyon Road south of Agoura Road. Over one hundred vendors had booths along the block-long route, displaying and selling handcrafted items such as jewelry, metalwork, and ceramics. Food and beverage vendors were also in attendance

Regent Westlake Theater at the County Line Shopping Center. (Courtesy Lussier Photography)

Buttercup School,
Russell Ranch Park.
(Courtesy Lussier
Photography)

and several music groups entertained the estimated crowd of fifty-five hundred adults and children who attended, despite overcast skies and cool weather.

The city awarded $20,000 in Community Service Grants and $5,000 in Cultural Grants to applicants selected by the Community Service Funds Allocation Committee appointed by the Council.

On March 26, the city discussed a letter from the Las Virgenes Unified School District (LVUSD) advising that ownership of the 1.34 acre land parcel on Foxfield Drive, adjacent to the Fire Station, would revert to the District unless the city had committed to some specific use for the site by mid-May. LVUSD wanted the site for possible use as a preschool location. The letter stated that if the city only committed to use the site without specifying the intended use, it "would be vulnerable to a challenge that the District would be compelled to bring. . . ." The city attorney disagreed with LVUSD's interpretation of the 1987 agreement, saying, "what the development agreement says is the city must decide whether it wishes to use the property. It does not say the city must use the property within the ten years." After some heated discussion, a spokesman for the School District advised they had not decided to take legal action. (The disputed property was given to the city in exchange for the rezoning of fifteen acres east of the site, so the District could sell it off to a housing developer for $5.3 million.)

After several weeks of intensive negotiation, a very creative agreement was reached in early May between the

Russell Ranch Park.

city and LVUSD under which the city would lease ten thousand square feet of land in the new Russell Ranch Park to the District for fifty-five years at one dollar a year. The District planned to build a federally mandated preschool on thirty-eight hundred square feet of the site and to use the balance as a play area.

Also on March 26, the Council took action to approve a "green waste" plan that would require all residents to separate their garden wastes and lawn clippings and place them in separate containers to be supplied by the collectors. The action was taken as a step toward meeting the state mandate of 50 percent diversion of waste from landfills by the year 2000.

In other actions in March, the Council approved the proposal by Northwest Atlantic Partners, an arm of Price-Costco, for the development to be

known as Westlake Marketplace. The sixteen-acre site, located north of the Price-Costco store, would accommodate 165,000 square feet of shops including three anchor stores, three fast-food restaurants, several smaller shops, and 741 parking spaces.

In late March, an emergency room physician advised the press that the opening of a twenty-four-hour emergency room by Tenet Healthcare had been delayed, although a letter of intent had been signed. It was also disclosed that Tenet was preparing a feasibility study on the possibility of opening a full-service hospital in Westlake Village, and had an option to purchase a hospital site.

On April 15, Zeneca Group PLC, a British pharmaceutical company, announced it had acquired all of Salick Healthcare operations in the United States. Zeneca had previously bought about half of Salick's businesses, and was exercising its option to purchase the balance. A Zeneca spokesman stated that no changes were contemplated for the Westlake operation.

In early May, the Council nominated Bonnie Gillespie as the selection for the city's outstanding senior at the county's Older Americans Recognition Day. Bonnie, a founding member in 1982 of Westlake Village Meals on Wheels and currently its president, was also a director of the New West Symphony. The county ceremonies included a luncheon and a presentation by the county supervisor.

With no progress reported on obtaining specifics on errant golf ball damage and insurance claims, the Council opted to reject the installation of a fence along the Agoura Road side of the Westlake Village Golf Course.

On June 12, the employees and doctors working at the Salick Healthcare Specialty Hospital were informed that the facility would be closed permanently by August 11 and that the property would be sold. As required by regulation, it had been reported to the state at the end of March that the operation had lost between $1.1 million and $1.6 million a month during the previous three quarters. The facility's executive director stated that the Salick Board made the decision, independent of Zeneca. It was expected that the closure would affect about seventy-five people, with some twenty-five to be relocated at other Salick facilities.

It was announced in late June that within sixty days, Columbia HCA would

Oaks Christian High School.

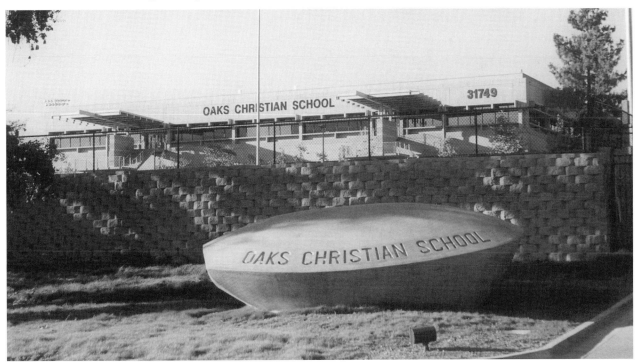

be buying back the Westlake Medical Center facility from Zeneca, the owner of Salick Healthcare. The price was not disclosed but one element of the deal was for Zeneca to drop the ongoing lawsuit against Columbia, which had been brought by Salick for claimed trade restrictions. A Columbia spokesman stated that Columbia had no current plans for the building once the sale took place.

Also in June, the Calvary Community Church announced it was in escrow to purchase the 310,000-square-foot industrial building on thirty-five acres fronting on La Tienda Drive and Via Rocas. The former Eaton Corporation building had been used for manufacture of sophisticated electronic warfare products and consequently included high security installations. In addition to the church, a Christian High School is to be developed by the Price Family Foundation on the property.

June and July saw a heating up of the arguments about an active sports park on Lot 79 adjacent to Westlake Canyon Oaks development. Many of the residents from that area protested the development of a park on the property but some others in the same area supported the concept. One resident of an adjacent development in Thousand Oaks became very active in opposing the park, later becoming actively involved in

a political campaign in Westlake Village. Many letters appeared in the local press, some in opposition, but others favoring the concept as much needed for the youth of the community—one of which was signed by presidents of twelve of the sixteen homeowners associations in the city. An attorney living in Thousand Oaks (with an office in Westlake Village), offered his services to an opposing group initiated by the nearby Thousand Oaks resident.

The Triunfo YMCA announced plans to build a twenty-thousand-square-foot facility on a lot on Lindero Canyon Road, which they had obtained at an advantageous price. There were immediate objections from some residents of Westlake Canyon Oaks because of concerns about traffic congestion and noise.

On July 9, the Council passed an ordinance limiting garage sales to one per year for each household. The action was taken because of complaints from neighbors about a home on Janlor Drive that was holding a sale every week, with clothing being delivered by truck from Los Angeles.

Again in July, the Council heard vociferous objections to an active park on Lindero Canyon Road, from residents on both sides of the county line.

In mid-July, the Los Angeles County Health Department, after a long delay, approved the use of ground water from Westlake Village wells for use in irrigation. The wells along Lindero Canyon Road produced water containing metal solvents making it unfit for other uses. The well water was to be piped to the District's Tapia water reclamation plant where it would be combined with other reclaimed water before distribution.

July 13, the last day for candidates to file for the upcoming City Council election, saw four interested citizens entering the race—incumbent Kris Carraway-Bowman was joined by newcomers Mark Rutherford, Iraj Broomand, and Christopher Mann.

On that same date the Sheriff's Department officially opened a field office in the Price-Costco building. Even though it was small, it contained a desk, chairs, a telephone, and lavatory facilities. Captain William J. McSweeney, commander of the Lost Hills Station, praised Price-Costco for donating the facility, and noted, "it improves response time and improves presence."

On July 18 there was a bomb scare at the office building next to Berniece Bennett Park. Ten Sheriff's vehicles responded and streets in the area were cordoned off while the Bomb Squad officers of the Sheriff's Arson and Explosives Unit investigated. The device, found on a chair in an empty office, looked very much like three sticks of dynamite with a timer attached but

turned out to be three tubes wired to a digital clock—someone's idea of a practical joke.

K-Swiss, a maker of high quality tennis shoes, officially announced in September the construction of its new corporate offices in the Spectrum Business Park. The large two-story building was expected to cost upwards of $6 million. The company, founded by Swiss skiers who took up tennis in the United States and designed their own all-leather footwear, reported income of $117 million in 1996.

In early October, State Assemblywoman Sheila Kuehl spoke to a large group of citizens, Council members and county officials at the Westlake Village City Hall. At the time she was serving as the speaker pro tem of the State Assembly and her appearance had been arranged by the Governmental Affairs Committee of the Westlake Village Chamber of Commerce. After a few opening comments, Assemblywoman Kuehl opened the meeting up to questions from the audience, which resulted in some fractious discussions.

In addition to a $536,000 widening plan for Lindero Canyon Road—paid for by the Westlake North developer—the Council decided to have a traffic light installed at Hedgewall Drive and Lindero Canyon Road. Even though traffic volumes and accidents were not up to the levels recommended by CALTRANS, the action was taken to install the $250,000 signal to ease traffic exiting from Westlake Canyon Oaks.

Election Day was November 4. After a vigorous campaign in which the proposal for an active park on Lot 79 and the need for a local hospital became major issues, the people made their choices. The 3,521 votes cast represented 68 percent of the city's electorate. The results were the election of three of the four candidates to the City Council. The vote counts were:

Broomand	1,234
Rutherford	1,148
Carraway-Bowman	1,139
Mann	761

November also saw the final approval by the Council of the new Calvary Community Church and the associated Price Family Foundation Christian High School.

On November 20, the State of the City luncheon was held at the Hyatt Westlake. Outgoing Mayor Douglas R. Yarrow presented a highly positive picture of the city's condition and future. He noted particularly that business was on an upswing, crime in the city was down materially, office vacancy was down to 6 percent and that Westlake North had become "the City's economic engine. . . ."

Five days later a dinner was held honoring both James E. Emmons and Douglas R. Yarrow for the years of service they had dedicated to the city,

New City Council, December 3, 1997. Left to right: Iraj Broomand, Mayor Kris Carraway-Bowman, James Henderson, Betty DeSantis, and Mark Rutherford. (Courtesy Lussier Photography)

both after two terms as City Council members and Emmons as an additional eight years as city manager. Both had announced earlier they would not be running for city office again. Many notables spoke of their contributions to the betterment and growth of the city. Additionally, both the honorees and the large audience who enjoyed some "roasting."

On December 3, Kris Carraway-Bowman was sworn in as the city's new mayor and Betty DeSantis took office as mayor pro tem. The two newly elected Council members, Mark Rutherford and Iraj Broomand, were also sworn in as Council members replacing the retiring Yarrow and Emmons.

1998

The year started out in a positive fiscal note during a '96–'97 audit review when the city treasurer and the outside auditors announced the city had a $5.3 million surplus. An increase of $400,000 in sales taxes, primarily from Costco and increased Transient Occupancy Tax (TOT) from the expanded Westlake Village Inn were important factors.

A groundbreaking ceremony was held on January 13 at the site for the new world headquarters of the Dole Food Company. CEO David H. Murdoch hosted the event, which was attended by many notables, including Governor Pete Wilson, Congressman Brad Sherman, and Mayor Kris Carraway-Bowman. Local officials were pleased with the governor's comments about the business friendly climate in Westlake Village. After speeches and presentations, all the dignitaries joined Dole's president, David De Lorenzo, in wielding the traditional gold shovels.

On February 11, the Council approved the Calvary Community Church plans for renovation and expansion of the thirty-five-acre former Eaton site on La Tienda Drive. Half of the facility is to be acquired by the Price Family Foundation for use as a Christian High School. Calvary is planning a three-thousand-seat Celebration Center, offices, classrooms, a bookstore, and other facilities, according to Pastor Larry DeWitt.

Final plans for the new world headquarters of the Dole Food Company were approved by the Council on March 11. The three-story building with 160,000 square feet of space was to be located on thirty acres at Lindero Canyon Road and Via Colinas. Underground parking, the first ever approved in the city, would accommodate two hundred vehicles.

In March, the controversy over a sports park on Lot 79 at the north end of the city again heated up. Letters to newspapers, comments from both nearby residents and nonresidents, the forming of a small organization by a nonresident calling itself the Neighborhood Preservation Group and the intercession of a well-known local attorney (willing to sue the city over it) all combined to exacerbate what many—other than immediate neighbors—considered a minor issue. During the rest of the year, considerable effort was expended on studies and EIRs for other potential park locations, primarily in Westlake North.

After making extensive plans for another Sunday Street Fair on Lakeview Canyon Road, the Rotary Board of Directors decided to cancel the event on Friday, March 27, after heavy rains and winds, associated with the El Nino weather arrived. However, Sunday dawned bright and clear—but no festival!

The city mailed survey forms in April to all households requesting preferences on locations for a new City Hall and Library. With 1,030 responses, 87 percent favored the Spectrum location for both facilities. And at an early May joint meeting of the Council and representatives from ten homeowner associations, there was unanimous support for the business park location.

Mid-April saw the opening of Albertson's, the first store at the Westlake Village Marketplace. Because the building was enclosed before the heavy rains of El Nino, interior work progressed and the

facility was ready for business some time before adjacent stores. The opening was attended by the company's CEO and representatives from the city and Chamber of Commerce.

At the May 13 Council meeting, Joyce Prouty, who with her husband Ray are the city historians, was proclaimed the city's nominee for Older Americans Recognition Day and as the honoree for Los Angeles County's Commission on Aging.

In late May, the Council approved a '98-'99 fiscal year budget of $3.62 million versus expected income of $4.5 million. Major contributors to income were sales and transient occupancy taxes, building permit fees, and income from a $6.7 million reserve.

On June 10, the Council finally made its official decision on the location for the proposed new City Hall and Library—the city-owned 3.9 acres of Lots 9 and 10 in the Spectrum Business Park.

Pinkerton, the worldwide security organization, signed a ten-year lease in early July on a seventy-thousand-square-foot building in the Spectrum Business Park. The company, which provides two hundred jobs in its world headquarters, is moving from the San Fernando Valley for a number of reasons, including the Los Angeles business tax. The city was part of the deal through an agreement to lease sixty parking spaces at the new City Hall–Library site for any Pinkerton overflow needs during daytime hours, with a reciprocal arrangement at night if needed.

Another element in the continuing saga of Baldwin-FDIC-SMMC-LVMWD-Westlake Vista arose in mid-August. The State Court of Appeals overturned the Los Angeles Superior Court's earlier decision to award Baldwin $11.2 million (later reduced to $4.2 million on the basis that Baldwin had already won a suit against the FDIC for $7 million).

The Council approved a solid waste collection agreement in August that provided a seven-year collection agreement with the two waste haulers currently serving the city. They were also required to provide three containers to each household to permit separation of recyclables, solid waste and green waste. These actions were taken to assist the city in meeting a 1989 state law requiring a 50 percent reduction in waste hauled to landfills by year 2000. The city also required the two haulers to convert to automated pick-up and to coordinate their pick-up days in each neighborhood.

With the understanding that the project would have to wait for installation of facilities, on September 11, the Council approved the construction of a crematorium and a maintenance building at Valley Oaks Memorial Park. The two facilities—the twelve-hundred-square-foot crematorium and the thirty-

six hundred-square-foot maintenance structure—would be constructed close to the rear of the property along the south leg of Russell Ranch Road and would be heavily screened by mature foliage.

By mid-September, the city had received eighteen proposals from architectural firms for the design of the new City Hall and Library. Each was a thick packet of qualifications, design examples, and related experience with municipal projects with price and schedule information. City staff was assigned the task of winnowing the quantity of bids down to a lesser number for the Council's study. A final decision was targeted for October.

After its extensive study of six proposals, the Council scheduled a four and one-half hour meeting to hear each of the firm's experiences with like projects and their concepts on the building's function and how its location would impact its form. A decision was reached to narrow the field to two companies—Fields Devereaux Architects and Engineers of Los Angeles and LPA of Irvine. There followed two full days of travel, visits to numerous projects and the offices of the two contenders by Council members and city staff. In subsequent review and discussions, the Council opted to open the search further by including CHCG Architects of Pasadena.

On October 21, members of the two local Chambers of Commerce voted overwhelmingly to merge the organizations. Thirty percent of the Thousand Oaks Chamber voted, favoring the move 243 to 3. With 39 percent of the Westlake Village Chamber voting, the count was 343 to 16. Janet Levett, president and C.E.O. of the Westlake group, announced the two Chambers hoped to complete the merger by November 1.

On November 19, Mayor Kris Carraway-Bowman presented her State of the City address to a large group at a luncheon in the Hyatt Westlake Hotel. She emphasized the many accomplishments by the city during the year—from selecting a site for the soon-to-be-built City Hall and Library complex to developing a city-sponsored program for children and teens.

By late November, the Las Virgenes Unified School District had given up its effort to buy an eleven-acre plot in Westlake North as a site for an elementary school, on which they had previously made an undisclosed offer to Richland Westlake, the property developers. The owner refused the offer and sold the land to Investment Development Services (IDS) for $9.7 million. It was later disclosed that the School District had offered $4 million. The district then studied the possibility of obtaining the property through condemnation after a decision by an arbitrator on the land value but in early December tabled the issue and took no action.

December 2 saw the "changing of the guard" at City Hall when outgoing Mayor Kris Carraway-Bowman turned the gavel over to the new mayor, Betty DeSantis. Carraway-Bowman spoke of her satisfaction with the site selection for the new City Hall and Library, which had been determined by a poll of city residents to which one-third had responded. Superior Court Judge Lawrence J. Mira swore in Mayor DeSantis and Mayor Pro Tem James Henderson.

The Urgent Care Center opened at the site of the old Westlake Medical Center on December 10 after a delay of a week waiting licensing approvals. The twenty-five-hundred-square-foot facility had been completely renovated and re-equipped to treat patients without life-threatening illnesses. It is staffed by emergency-trained doctors and registered nurses, and includes nine stations and three beds.

1999

In early January, the City Land Use Committee met with officials of the Triunfo YMCA to review a revised plan for a $4 million fitness club on the four acres of Lot 80 on Lindero Canyon Road. The updated plan called for a twenty-three-hundred-square-foot building to include two pools, a gymnasium, a weight exercise room, locker rooms, and offices. The Committee expressed concerns about traffic safety and suggested that the applicant study means of ameliorating such potential problems, particularly at morning and evening rush hours.

Another building proposal came before the Land Use Committee in early January, when Castle and Cooke, the real estate arm of the Dole Food Company, presented a revised hotel and office structure plan. The structures, to be located on the lower part of Dole's thirty-acre property, would include a 90,000-square-foot hotel with 152 rooms, a 19,200-square-foot spa, a 180,000-square-foot office building, and a 720-car underground parking garage.

On January 16, after extensive reviews, the Council selected CHCG Architects of Pasadena to design the city's new City Hall and Library facility. That decision was made after visits by Council members to a number of CHCG-designed structures, including the City Hall in Culver City, and numerous visits to their offices with principals Armando Gonzalez and David Goodale.

In late January, the city was recognized in the 1999 Kosmont Business Survey as one of the "top ten" jurisdictions in Southern California that offer businesses a "very low cost" of operating. The city manager pointed out that since its inception in 1981, the city has taken a business-friendly position, with no business license fees, receipts, or utilities taxes.

A revised EIR on the proposed Lot 79 park on north Lindero Canyon Road was released on January 27. Even though it was based on a greatly reduced plan, in both size and facilities from the original proposal, criticism of the proposed plan was immediate. A pro bono attorney for the group, Neighborhood Preservation Group, said collection of signatures would start soon to require a special election on the matter.

In February, the Council approved a 134,000-square-foot office building to be located on the east side of Russell Ranch Road south of the Renaissance housing development. The applicant, Industrial Development Services (IDS) then was granted approval in April for two more buildings on the west side of Russell Ranch Road. Each structure would be two stories tall, totaling 190,000 square feet on the eleven acres, which the Las Virgenes Unified School District had at one time attempted to acquire.

Tuesday, March 3, saw the first eight people on the staff of the Calvary Community Church move into new quarters at the almost-completed new two-hundred-thousand-square-foot sanctuary on La Tienda Drive. Church officials hoped to have the move completed in time for Palm Sunday services on March 28 and Easter Sunday, April 4.

The Council held a special meeting on April 29 to hear the public's comments and suggestions regarding the new City Hall and Library design and layout. While only twenty citizens showed up and none were opposed to the project, some questions were raised about the size of the Library complex but few other suggestions were made.

On May 24 the Council honored two residents for their work in the community. Diana Malmquist was named Citizen of the Year for her extensive volunteer activities—with

cancer patients, as an active member of the Wellness Community, and chairman for five years of the Holiday Homes Tour for the same organization, as a thirty-year volunteer with the Conejo Valley Days celebration and as a member of numerous city committees. Patrick Yarrow, eighteen, a student at Crespi High School, was named Youth of the Year. The YMCA nominated Yarrow for his leadership and participation as president of a "Youth and Government." He headed the local delegation to Sacramento where youth basically take over state government for a day.

At the same meeting, another volunteer and community activist, Virginia Drasnin, was named Westlake

City Council members, December 8, 1999. Left to right: Chris Carroway-Bowman, Mark Rutherford, Mayor Iraj Broomand, Betty DeSantis, and Chris Mann. (Courtesy Lussier Photography)

Village's Older American of the Year. As such, she joined others at a recognition luncheon at the Dorothy Chandler Pavilion, hosted by the County of Los Angeles where she was again feted.

Lot 79 was again in the news when, on April 14 the Council voted 4-0 to approve the final Environmental Impact Report on the proposed park. That decision was taken only after many hours of public input and questioning of staff members. It was noted that approval of the EIR did not guarantee the approval of the park. Despite attempts to limit comments to the matter at hand—the EIR approval—some of the more than one hundred people attending insisted on digressing from the subject and on voicing negative opinions about the possible existence of a park in the future. The few who spoke in favor of a park were loudly booed and hissed—an unusual event for a Westlake Village Council meeting.

The hospital issue heated up toward the end of summer, simultaneously with the start of the political season. Many letters with accusations, innuendoes, and personal attacks appeared in the local press. Attempts by the local Council of Governments (COG), initiated by the Westlake Village Council, to obtain financial support from the county for purchase of hospital land resulted in an extensive study by the Los Angeles County Chief Administrative Officer's staff. That evaluation concluded that hospital and emergency service in the area was better than county standards and in any event, county funds were needed for the indigent. The Council had previously sent letters to twelve of the largest hospital operators in the country in attempts to find one that would be willing to consider opening a hospital in the area. All responses were negative.

In early September, the location for the proposed and revised YMCA again became an issue—primarily because of concerns about traffic, noise, and light pollution expressed by nearby residents. The Council approved a $30,000 contract with Cotton-Beland Associates of Pasadena for a study of the environmental impacts the project could have on surrounding residential areas. The report was to also identify alternate sites for the project, one of which had already been reviewed unofficially. The YMCA officials had indicated that a site along Thousand Oaks Boulevard, west of Lindero Canyon Road would be acceptable, if a land swap could be worked out with the owners—the Westlake Canyon Oaks Homeowner Association.

Also in September, Raypak, Inc., manufacturer of boilers and heating equipment, announced its plans to move its facility to Oxnard. Raypak, one of the original large businesses in Westlake

Village had occupied the Agoura Road site since 1970 but now found it had outgrown the location, purchased property in Oxnard where land was available for $4 to $5 per square foot, whereas Westlake Village prices were about $20 a square foot. They also announced plans to build the new $14 million facility to accommodate their need for expansion.

At the November 2 election for the two open Council seats, early and unofficial vote counts showed incumbent Betty DeSantis holding a commanding lead with 896 votes, or 40.9 percent of those voting, whereas Chris Mann and James Henderson were one vote apart—Mann with 631 votes and Henderson with 632. Final and vote counts and a recount on November 22 showed Mann had won with 756 votes to Henderson's 736—a twenty-vote margin.

In early November, the Council approved the $52,000 contract with the City of Agoura Hills as funding for local youth to participate for the third year in the Teen Recreation Program, based in Agoura Hills. The numerous programs operated year-round, had proved to be highly successful in attracting a large number of Westlake Village young people between ten and fifteen years of age.

December 8 was the transition date for the City Council. Iraj Broomand was voted in as mayor for the coming year,

and Chris Mann took the oath with outgoing Mayor Betty DeSantis as newly elected Council Members. James Henderson received accolades for his services to the community.

2000

Officials from cities along the 101 corridor met on January 26 with representatives from the California Department of Transportation (CALTRANS) and the Metropolitan Transportation Agency (MTA) to discuss the problems and possible solutions for traffic congestion on the 101 Freeway from the Ventura County line to the San Fernando Valley. It was noted that the two hundred thousand vehicle trips per day would increase by about 80 percent over the next twenty-five years. The MTA, which funnels state and federal monies for highway projects, emphasized that more in-depth study, which they would pay for, would be required before the area could qualify for any construction funding. Some participants expressed dissatisfaction with that approach, noting that the problems were obvious. Other suggestions included the installation of carpool lanes but it was noted that state legislation passed in the mid-1960s prohibited them on Highway 101. (The Las Virgenes–Malibu Council of Governments approved a $4.5 million study of the traffic patterns along 101 in late May. The study was expected to take two years.)

In late January, the Council approved an appeal of the state mandate through the Southern California Association of Governments (SCAG) requiring that Westlake Village provide for 315 more housing units in the General Plan. Under the law, 84 of those units must be priced for very low- or low-income families over the next five years. The issue had been the subject of discussion numerous times, with the city taking the position that the state's estimates of the requirements were based on 1990 census figures on home counts and that there was not enough available and affordable land.

Also in late January, the City Council honored two outstanding citizens for their accomplishments as volunteers and community activists. Amir Nejad, an Agoura High School senior was cited as "Youth of the Year" and Debby Gustafson was named "Citizen of the Year." Nejad, an accomplished tennis player and speaker of five languages, had dedicated his time to coaching Special Olympics, to the Future Business Leaders of America, the city's Park Advisory Committee, and other community services. Gustafson received her award for her dedication to the city's Disaster Response Team. She had been a driving force in establishing

the Team in Westlake Village and had devoted much of her time to its growth and success. Many hours of her time had been spent on training other members, on public education and on maintaining the large inventory of emergency supplies and equipment.

The plans for parking at the new civic center were changed February 9, when the architects, Gonzalez and Goodale, advised the Council of the existence of expansive soil in the area planned for a two-story $1.4 million parking structure. With an additional $430,000 estimated for stabilization, the Council opted instead to approve a one-level parking area, even though it would bring parking twenty-five feet closer to the center courtyard.

On April 12, the Council approved the recommendations of two committees on the distribution of funds to nonprofit and cultural organizations serving the city's residents. twenty-six of the nonprofits, which had requested a total of $100,000, shared a total of $30,000 while the cultural groups received $5,000. The major award of $7,000 went to the Friends of the Westlake Village Library.

Triunfo YMCA officials announced in late April that they were ready to go before the Council to request approval of their planned thirty-thousand-square-foot building on Lindero Canyon Road. All environmental impact studies had been completed and the YMCA principals hoped to start construction as soon as city approval was granted. In mid-June, however, a lawsuit was filed by the Westlake Canyon Oaks Homeowners Association against North Ranch Gateway Shopping Center, alleging that the property actually belonged to their Association. The lawsuit effectively terminated discussions on a land swap, which would allow building the facility on Thousand Oaks Boulevard west of the car wash property. It was also noted that the Lindero Canyon Road property did not belong to the North Ranch Gateway but to a family trust. By September, the Association had dropped the lawsuit, citing increasing costs and a survey that did not show strong support by the homeowners.

Kenneth E. Rufener, former mayor and councilman and thirty-three-year resident of Westlake Village, was presented with a plaque recognizing his nomination for the Older Americans Recognition Day. At the May 10 ceremonial luncheon at the Dorothy Chandler Pavilion he was presented with a scroll from the Los Angeles County Board of Supervisors.

The second annual Great Conejo Duck Race was held on Sunday, June 11.

128 City Council members, December 6, 2000. Left to right: Chris Mann, Chris Carroway-Bowman, Mayor Mark Rutherford, Betty DeSantis, and Iraj Broomand.

About twelve thousand three-inch rubber ducks, some wearing sunglasses, were turned loose on the two-hundred-yard course in Westlake Lake. The winner sped to the finish line in only twenty-five minutes, winning numerous prizes for its sponsor. More than $35,000 was raised to benefit both Many Mansions and the Otto Stoll Children's Fund.

The Council approved the new budget for the 2000–2001 fiscal year on June 14. General Fund expenditures were listed at $5.27 million, up about $370,000 from the prior year. That increase was more than balanced by an expected increase in reserves of about $750,000, bringing the total city reserves to an all-time high of $9 million.

The Council's Hospital Ad Hoc Committee assigned the task of investigating means of bringing a hospital to the area was disbanded in late July. That action was taken after about four years of fruitless efforts to interest hospital corporations to build in the area. Lack of interest by other cities in the regional Council of Governments was also cited.

On September 3, a memorial tree was planted on the greenbelt in First Neighborhood in honor of John R. Schauerman. Up to the time of his passing "Jack," a longtime resident, had served on the First Neighborhood Board of Directors for over a decade, primarily as treasurer, where his "less than 2 percent variation" budgets attested to his dedication to the assignment.

The Council denied a request by JBH Development Company to open the end of the Yellowwood Drive cul-de-sac in Three Springs on October 25. The developer stated that such access was required across the county line to permit construction of nine homes. Similar requests for access had been refused by the city previously.

Early November saw the approval by the Council of major additions and modifications to the Westminster Presbyterian Church. The twenty-two-thousand-square-foot additions will allow for expansion of the sanctuary, a new narthex, expansion of the preschool, the administration building, and the fellowship hall as well as an education building. The city's traffic and parking concerns were also addressed and resolved.

The city's annual reorganization meeting was held on December 6. Mark Rutherford was elected mayor for the coming year as Iraj Broomand stepped down from that post. Kris Carraway-Bowman was appointed mayor pro tem. Rutherford stated his primary goals were to ensure that the new City Hall and Library project would proceed smoothly and to increase police protection because of burglaries and continually climbing road speeds in the past year.

2001: Into the New Millennium

2001

The year opened with a 4-0 vote by the Council to approve an agreement with Oaks Christian High School which will permit use of the school's sports fields by public groups. In this rare example of "church and state" coordination, the city will lend the school up to $615,000 to be repaid in ten years, including 9.1 percent interest.

For the second time, Castle and Cooke—the independent real estate arm of the Dole Food Company—announced in January plans to build a "world class" 182-room hotel with a freestanding spa on the property south of Dole's World Headquarters building. A separate five-story office building was also planned, with most of the first story below ground level.

Because of the state's energy crunch, in February Southern California Edison announced the probability of rolling blackouts that would affect the Westlake Village area. They also urged conservation by both businesses and homeowners to minimize the need for such actions, pointing out that the California Independent System Operator, as an independent agency, directs orders for such actions.

In late February, the local Council of Governments (COG) representing the Cities of Westlake Village, Agoura Hills, Hidden Hills, Malibu, and Calabasas announced it had been instrumental in obtaining sufficient funding to study traffic solutions for the 101 Freeway, including the portion from the Route 23 Freeway in Thousand Oaks to downtown Los Angeles. The study, which is expected to take three years, has been allocated 4.5 million dollars. Problems posed by the 230,000 vehicle trips each day using that part of the freeway at an average speed of twenty to thirty miles per hour are expected to worsen with time. Some criticisms were voiced regarding the need for "another study" of an obvious problem but it was noted that it is a necessary precursor to obtaining expansion funding under federal guidelines.

At the March 14 meeting, the Council honored two residents for their service to the community. Karl Balke was recognized as Citizen of the Year. As president of the Oak Forest Estates Homeowners Association, Balke for years had worked with his association members and others on preservation of the native oak trees. He received a commemorative plaque and the city donated $500 to a charity of his choice.

The Youth of the Year Award recognized Raman Rajagopal as the outstanding youth of the community for his many accomplishments and honors. Among those were the presidency of the Agoura High School Student Union, the Honor Roll at his school, AP Scholar with Honors, and Board member of the Inter-Community Student Council.

On March 26, the results of the School Site Employees Bonus program were announced. The state-mandated Academic Performance Index tests results for each school and determines its eligibility for the award. White Oak Elementary School was awarded $62,337, half of which is paid to employees of the school and half goes to school site grants.

In late March, the Westlake Canyon Oaks Homeowners Association sent ballots to all members to poll them on a land swap that would grant acreage in their Lot 77, fronting on Thousand Oaks Boulevard, in exchange for Lot 80, the current proposed site for the new YMCA. Association rules require a two-thirds affirmative vote to approve the swap.

On March 27, the Council appointed a Grand Opening Committee to plan for the long-awaited events that would mark the official start of operations in the new City Hall and Library. Diana Malmquist was appointed chairman of the group, which had a year to complete the task.

The Westlake Rotary Club held its street fair on Sunday, April 1, at the usual location on Lakeview Canyon Road. Many thousands enjoyed the food, entertainment, and the numerous crafts on display in dozens of booths. Sponsored by many local companies, profits from the event were all donated to local nonprofit organizations.

The Council voted a donation of $60,000 to Senior Concerns on April 2 and $50,000 of the fund will be used for the much needed expansion of the Fitzgerald Senior Day Support Center on Hodencamp Road in Thousand Oaks. The balance of $10,900 is to help support the Center's programs for the memory-impaired and frail elderly. The new addition will almost double the size of the facility and construction is expected to be completed in 2002.

With monies provided by the state of California to cities for improvement of traffic enforcement, two motorcycle officers were added to the Lost Hills Sheriff's Station roster in early April. The estimated $220,000 annual cost of continued operation will be funded by the five cities served by Lost Hills.

On April 24, a reproduction of an El Camino Real Bell was dedicated at a ceremony in First Neighborhood's Freedom Square. The Westlake Village Women's Club initiated the activity to commemorate the route of the area's pioneers, in coordination with the Automobile Club and the city.

Eleanor Roche of Thousand Oaks and Betty DeSantis of Westlake Village received the prestigious Golden Heart Awards from the American Heart Association. They were honored at the Association's twelfth annual Spring Gala at the Hyatt Westlake Hotel on May 5 because of their numerous contributions to health and education on behalf of the organization.

The body of an unidentified man was removed from the Westlake Reservoir by the Sheriff's Department's Air-5 rescue helicopter on May 24. It was at first suspected that the victim was a man reported missing from Malibu. The body lacked outer clothing, and the helicopter searched the area unsuccessfully for such items. The body was later identified.

On Monday, May 28, the traditional Memorial Day celebration was held at Valley Oaks Memorial Park. Ceremonies included tableaus of American military history, a concert by the Air National Guard Band, songs covering two hundred years of American history by the one hundred voices of the Amen Chorus of the Shepherd of the Hills Church and a flyover of a squadron of World War II aircraft.

Spring and summer this year saw a great shortage of electric power generation in the state. Costs skyrocketed as natural gas prices—the main energy source for the state's power generators— soared to very high levels. Rationing of power became the order of the day for major power consuming industries. Citizens were urged to turn down air conditioners, turn out unneeded lights, and otherwise conserve electricity wherever possible. Periodic blackouts occurred in many areas of the state but only three times in the local area and then for only short periods. By the end of summer, most problems had been solved and full service was again available. However, City Hall stayed on its 7 a.m. to 4 p.m. schedule to continue power conservation.

Sunday, June 10, was the date for the annual Great Conejo Duck Race on Westlake Lake. The rubber ducks were sponsored at $5 each (or $25 for a "Six Quack") by over one hundred businesses and many individuals. Proceeds, expected to top $25,000, were for the benefit of Many Mansions, a nonprofit group that helps to provide housing for low-income families in the Conejo area. Three ducks were designated as "Million Dollar Ducks." If any of them came in first, their sponsor would win one million dollars. All three ducks finished "back in the pack."

The Council declared Kaitlin Wilson the winner in the contest to develop a logo for the city's twentieth anniversary. Kaitlin, a fifth grade student at St. Jude's Elementary School, developed the

estlake Village - "It's Right Up There"

winning design, featuring the slogan "Westlake Village—it's right up there."

In a decision on a case several years old, the California Supreme Court issued a ruling in June that impacted the city's 1990 increase in Transient Occupancy Tax (TOT) from 6 percent to 10 percent. The court found that any such taxes imposed between 1985 and 1995 without a vote of the electorate were open to challenges. In late July, the Council decided to put the issue to the voters in the November election.

The issue of a hospital in the Westlake Village area surfaced once again in early July as an election issue— despite some protests that it was not. A candidate in a nearby city declared the existing area hospital inadequate to handle the region's needs. An incumbent whose first election had stressed the need for another and closer facility refused to disclose details of an independent group claimed to have promises of financial support. The discussion closed with a 3–1 vote to re-establish the Ad Hoc Committee to review the issue and to coordinate with counterparts in Thousand Oaks and other nearby cities.

On July 1, Los Angeles County Sheriff Lee Baca appointed Lieutenant (now Captain) James Glazer, a longtime and respected operations officer at the Lost Hills Sheriff's Station, as commander of that facility. Glazer had actually assumed those duties when his predecessor, Captain John O'Brien had gone on medical leave the previous November.

The traditional Fourth of July parade under the auspices of the Westlake Village Junior Women's Club was again a big success. Starting as usual, at the parking lot of the Westlake Hospital facility on Lakeview Canyon Road, the long line of patriotically decorated bicycles, carriages, coaster wagons, and strollers proceeded east along Agoura Road, under the protection of Sheriff's deputies. The route turned south on Greengate Court and ended in Berniece Bennett Park. Free balloons were available, along with refreshments and face painting for the children.

The Council approved the plan on July 11 to convert the open Foxfield site, opposite the St. Jude's Church, to a community park. A picnic shelter, located near the adjacent Fire Station was included in the plan, as well as a basketball half-court. A Tot Lot was relocated further from the street and enlarged to accommodate more equipment. A meandering trail was also included, screened from nearby residences by many trees.

Left: City's twentieth anniversary logo designed by Kaitlin Wilson, fifth grade student at St. Jude's Elementary School.

133

SEPTEMBER 11: Along with the rest of the country, Westlake Village residents recoiled in shock and outrage at the heinous terrorist attacks and the great loss of lives in New York, Washington, D.C., and Pennsylvania. A renewed sense of patriotism and support for government action became quickly evident.

SEPTEMBER 13: People wanted flags to show support for victims and rescue workers, but very few were available. Paula Weiser of Weiser Litho on La Baya Drive asked her creative staff to design a poster immediately that would express the feelings of the public. A 17″ by 22″ poster was designed—a rippling flag with the message "United We Stand." Copies were rolling off the press that afternoon and by 4 p.m. on Friday over eight thousand had been given away to schools, government offices, and businesses. Response was over-whelming. Within days, requests for copies came from Sacramento, the White House, England, Italy, Germany, South Korea, and many walk-in celebrities. The press ran over one hundred thousand copies. Paper and ink suppliers donated their materials and many contributions were received, all of which were sent to disaster relief agencies.

UNITED WE STAND

REMEMBERING
• SEPTEMBER 11, 2001 •
OUR HEARTS AND OUR PRAYERS GO OUT TO THE VICTIMS, RESCUE WORKERS AND ALL AMERICANS AFFECTED BY THIS COWARDLY ACT OF TERRORISM.

In late July, the Council approved fees for the joint-use sports fields at Oaks Christian High School. The facilities include a baseball field, a softball field, and two soccer/football fields. Depending upon the fields used, rates would either be $10 per hour unlighted and $20 an hour when lighted. Staff members estimated income from those fees of $30,000 to $40,000 a year.

By late August, five people had taken out papers to run for City Council in November. Incumbents Mark Rutherford and Iraj Broomand were joined by newcomers Susan McSweeney, Robert Slavin, and Ronald Klamert. Mayor Pro Tem Kris Carraway-Bowman had previously announced her decision not to run for a third term.

On Sunday September 9, Dale Kristien who for some years sang a leading role in Phantom of the Opera, presented a concert at Berniece Bennett Park. Accompanied by Elmer Ramsey's Conejo Pops Orchestra, Kristien performed music from her album The Beauty of Broadway. The concert, presented as part of the city's twentieth anniversary celebration, was enthusiastically received by a very large group of families.

In late September, the YMCA was still planning to move ahead with its new facility on Lindero Canyon Road, when negotiations with the Westlake Canyon Oaks Homeowners Association were resumed on a possible land swap.

An open property on Thousand Oaks Boulevard had been suggested as an alternate site and the majority of the homeowners had approved the exchange in the spring. That plan had been put on hold when the Association Board members could not reach agreement on how much of the fifty-five acres of that land should be included.

November 6 was Election Day. The preceding weeks had seen a plethora of campaign signs for the five City Council candidates—more than any prior Council elections. All candidates had attended rallies and expressed their views at community forums. The final vote tallies, available late that Tuesday night, showed that two newcomers and one holdover had been selected for the four-year terms.

Bob Slavin	1,140
Mark Rutherford	1,004
Susan McSweeney	934
Iraj Broomand	691
Ron Klamert	326

At the same election, the voters were asked to decide on two propositions. Item "T" asked for approval to legitimatize prior Council action, which had raised the Transient Occupancy Tax ("Bed Tax") from 6 percent to 10 percent. Item "U" asked for another 4 percent raise (to 14 percent) to be applied at a later date when and if the Council deemed it necessary.

The results were:

	Yes	No
Item "T"—	1,084	431
Item "U"—	456	1,047

On November 10, the city officially celebrated its twentieth anniversary with a black tie–optional cocktail reception and dinner at North Ranch Country Club. Mayor Mark Rutherford briefly addressed the nearly two hundred attending, and recognition was given to six of the city's founding members. The high point of the evening was a video presentation of comments from a number of people who were or had been involved with the city. The audience was particularly amused when a number of outtakes from the taping were shown. Fran Targon chaired the very successful event, with able assistance from Betty DeSantis, Justine Maderos, Tony Tramonto, and others.

The traditional State of the City luncheon was held on November 16, sponsored as in the past by the Chamber of Commerce at the Hyatt Westlake Hotel. Fog machines, flash lighting, and a darkened room surprised guests as they arrived with scenes from *2001—A Space Odyssey* being shown on large screens. Music from that same epic set the tone for a year-by-year commentary by Mayor Mark Rutherford on the city's history, "2001—A City Odyssey," accompanied by many pictures on the dual screens. The city's excellent financial condition and progress on the construction of the new City Hall and Daniel K. Ludwig Library were also reviewed.

On Wednesday, December 5, Superior Court Judge Lawrence A. Mira once again donned his robes to swear in the three newly elected Council members. Mayor Pro Tem Kris Carraway-Bowman, who had chosen not to run for a third term on the Council, was lauded by her Council associates and by representatives from other cities, the county, and the federal government. With tears, she thanked her husband for the continuing support he had given during her terms in office. Iraj Broomand also expressed his appreciation to his supporters and fellow Council members as his term ended.

Ceremonies followed in which Betty DeSantis, for the second time, was elected mayor for the coming year and Chris Mann was voted mayor pro tem. DeSantis spoke about goals for the coming year, including completion and inauguration of the new City Hall–Library complex, as well as the Foxfield Park.

2002

At the first meeting of the year, the City Council approved a Single-Family Housing Rehabilitation Plan that would provide guidelines and procedures for allocation of up to $5,000 per household for repairs. Qualification for such grants is based on income level and the need for repairs, which would affect safety or health.

On January 20, the Council met to discuss goals for the city in the year 2002. Twenty items suggested by the Council Members were reviewed, discussed, and were either posted for action by staff or a committee, or deferred to a later date.

Early in the year, the California Transportation Authority (CALTRANS) announced the start of a $4.5 million study of the traffic situation and possible methods of alleviation on the Ventura Freeway, from Route 23 in Thousand Oaks to downtown Los Angeles. The freeway now serves about 1.5 million population along its route, with an expected increase to 1.9 million by 2025. The new study is said to be more comprehensive than other studies in the past. Those studies had indicated an average speed of twenty to thirty miles per hour for the quarter million vehicles traveling the route each day.

Also in January, the city denied a lawsuit brought by relatives of a man unfortunately killed while crossing Townsgate Road. Their attorney was advised that the location is within the City of Thousand Oaks, even though he claimed to have been advised otherwise.

With the current lease expiring on January 31, the City Hall offices were moved on Saturday, January 26, to the new Westlake Village Civic Center at Agoura Road and Oak Crest Drive—just a block from the old location. The move was supervised by just two of the city staff members and was completed on that date.

On January 30, the first Council meeting was held in the new Civic Center facility. Among the several items discussed and passed by the Council was a statement of support for Proposition 42. That item on the upcoming ballot in March would continue to allow sales taxes on gasoline to be used for road repairs and maintenance.

At ceremonies on Friday evening, February 8, the local Chamber of Commerce honored Kris Carraway-Bowman as Woman of the Year. She was cited for her many activities with local charities, her service on Boards of Heart and Cancer organizations and her eight-year service as a City Council member in Westlake Village, during which she served a term as mayor.

February was a month of urgency for the contractors working to complete the many unfinished items, particularly in the new Council chambers and community rooms. With the City Hall staff already moved into the new facility, some temporary accommodations had to be made. Council meetings were held in the large, unfinished conference room. Temporary plywood tops were installed on the counters in the main lobby. The contractor for the forecourt water feature was terminated and a new company was hired. The Council chambers were much behind schedule, as was the landscaping.

At their March 13 meeting, the Council unanimously approved a contract with Donning Company/Publishers for production of two thousand copies of a "coffee table" book on the history of the area both before and after city incorporation.

Saturday, March 23, dawned partly cloudy with the threat of light showers. The entire crew of volunteers for the opening day celebrations of City Hall and the Library was on hand to arrange the decorations—balloons and flowers—and to set up grills for food, tables for beverages and sandwiches, and other tables for attendees. With all the decorations contributed by many local supermarkets, florists, and balloon stores, the entire building and grounds had a very festive look appropriate to the occasion.

By 11:00 a. m., many hundreds of people had arrived and were seated in front of a raised, canopied stage. After a greeting and introductory remarks by Mayor Betty DeSantis, Boy Scout Troops 485 and 775 conducted the Presentation of Colors. The "Pledge of Allegiance" was led by members of Boy Scout Troop 745, after which the children of White Oak Elementary School sang "God Bless America." Dr. Robert C. Bos, the retired pastor of Westminster Presbyterian Church, gave the invocation. Councilwoman Susan McSweeney introduced former Council members, officials from the Los Angeles County Fire Department, the County Sheriff's Department, the Las Virgenes Unified School District, the Las Virgenes Municipal Water District, and the Thousand Oaks-Westlake Village Regional Chamber of Commerce.

A history of the new edifice was given by Councilman Mark Rutherford, from the initial consideration of whether to build it, where to build it, selection of an architect, a soils analyst, a construction company, a project management team, and the actual construction process.

The mayor greeted the many dignitaries who had attended to help celebrate the occasion. Los Angeles County Supervisor and Chairman of the Board of Supervisors Zev Yaroslavsky presented a plaque from Los Angeles County. Other plaques and proclamations were presented by State Assemblywoman Fran Pavley, Larry Horner for Congressman Brad Sherman, Laura Plotkin for State Senator Sheila Kuehl, and Margaret Todd, the county librarian.

Mayor Pro Tem Chris Mann then presented special awards to the team that made it all happen—the architects Armando Gonzalez and David Goodale,

the builder Viola Inc., the program management team from Swinerton Management Corporation and Linda Demmers, the library consultant.

A ribbon-cutting ceremony then was held—with many pictures—to mark the official opening. At that point Mel Flack's Riverboat Dixie Band took over the stage and entertained the crowd with many Dixieland renditions. Most people took advantage of the opportunity to visit the city offices, the as-yet incomplete Council chambers, the community rooms (where many signed up to acquire copies of "A City in the Country": A History of the City of Westlake Village. At the beautiful Daniel K. Ludwig Library visitors were entertained by the harp renditions of Melanie Griffith and by David Freeman on flute. The well-known group, The Village Voices, entertained visitors to the City Hall.

Much credit goes to the city staff for their contributions to the success of the opening day—particularly Audrey J. Brown, the assistant city manager. Much assistance and a gracious ambiance for the guests were provided by the docents—twenty young ladies each from Lindero Middle School and Agoura High School.

It was a most memorable day that marks the end of this narrative chronicle —and a high point in the history of the City of Westlake Village.

Section II

COMMUNITY FEATURES
AND SERVICES

THE HOUSES OF WORSHIP

It is only fitting that these individual histories start with the numerous religious institutions that have over the years provided spiritual support for the people of the community.

It is noted that the first religious services in Westlake Village were conducted in White Oak Elementary School and First Neighborhood Community Center. Catholic, Lutheran, Presbyterian, and Methodist faiths all used those facilities and the Jewish congregation used White Oak Elementary for its religious school.

Accommodating all those groups required a very considerable amount of planning and scheduling by the leaders of each faith—and that cooperative propinquity soon resulted in the formation of the Ecumenical Council.

St. Jude's Catholic Church

In early 1970, the Los Angeles Archdiocese recognized the growing need in the fast-expanding Westlake Village area and assigned Father Thomas O'Connell to establish a parish. On July 1, 1970, with the participation

of thirty-five local families, St. Jude's was officially founded. The first daily masses were said in a chapel in Father O'Connell's home across the street from White Oak Elementary School. Sunday masses were held at 8:30 a.m. at the First Neighborhood Community Center—a facility shared at that time with the new Presbyterian, Methodist, and Lutheran congregations.

Prior to the Triunfo Ranch sale to American-Hawaiian in 1963, certain parcels of land had been deeded to the Los Angeles Archdiocese. One of them, about ten acres, was located within the area being planned for what was to become First Neighborhood. Subsequent negotiations, circa 1964, resulted in an exchange of other American-Hawaiian properties for that ten acres, and among them were the four acres at the southwest corner of what were to become Lindero Canyon Road and Foxfield Drive.

Father O'Connell and his parishioners soon started to plan and raise money for a permanent church and in 1971 the first building was erected on the four-acre church grounds. That structure housed a sanctuary for the Sunday mass, and various other rooms, with moveable walls, for religious education, offices, and a kitchen. The year 1974 saw the addition of two more classrooms and the enlarging of the parking lot. Upon completion of that project, work was started on a new rectory and upon its completion in 1975, Father O'Connell moved from his house on Village School Road.

in time for the 1985-1986 school year. By 2000, a new science lab and an expanded library were required to serve the student body of over three hundred.

St. Jude's Catholic Church.

As the congregation grew under the ministry of "Father Tom," it became necessary to start planning and raising funds for a permanent church. Plans for the sanctuary were drawn up in 1979 and in 1981 the present church became a reality. The first mass in the new facility was celebrated on Mother's Day in 1981 and the following November, Cardinal Timothy Manning, archbishop of the Los Angeles Archdiocese, officiated at the dedication and consecration ceremonies.

St. Jude's K-8 school was opened on September 7, 1982, and in May 1984 groundbreaking was held for new school buildings. Construction was started in August of that year and was completed

In recognition of his very successful stewardship, in November 1993, Father O'Connell was notified by the Vatican of his elevation to Monsignor. In February 1994, Cardinal Manning conducted the official investiture. After a brief retirement, "Father Tom" passed away in February 1998, leaving his parish that had grown to almost four thousand families.

Temple Adat Elohim

The first Jewish Reform Temple in the area had its beginnings on August 22, 1967, at a formation meeting of sixteen families. Exactly one-month later student Rabbi Gary Dolin conducted the first services at Hidden Trail Camp in Agoura. Originally designated as the Reform Temple of Conejo Valley, it received its Hebrew name, Temple *Adat Elohim* ("Congregation of God") on February 8, 1968. In August 1969, student Rabbi Gary Dolin left for Israel and Rabbi Fred Krinsky, on leave from his chairmanship of the Political Science Department at USC, became the spiritual leader. Also in 1969, the Temple received its Torah, which had been rescued from the Nazis and restored in England.

Interior of Temple Adat Elohim.

Major changes for the Temple and its congregation were to take place in 1972. Rabbi Krinsky felt it was time to leave and the congregation had grown large enough to require a full-time Rabbi. Rabbi Edward Zerin came to the congregation and soon the Temple, crowded for room, moved to its new location at Covenant House in Westlake Village. (Covenant House was the sanctuary shared by the United Methodist Church and the Westlake Lutheran Church—see history of the United Methodist Church.)

The religious school of the Temple also had a number of venues—at Westlake Elementary School, Triunfo Elementary School, and White Oak Elementary School—before settling in at Covenant House.

In 1976, the Temple presented a plaque to Covenant House proclaiming "HI-NE-MAT-TOV-UMA-NA-IM," meaning "How good it is, and how pleasant when brethren dwell together in unity."

In 1977, the congregation, still growing, approved plans to purchase a former church site in Thousand Oaks on Hillcrest Drive. On September 29, the Temple departed Westlake Village as the congregation carried the Torahs through the streets of Westlake and Thousand Oaks and placed them in the new Temple building. Since that time a new sanctuary and social hall have been built on the site. The sanctuary alone can seat four hundred and when the partition to the social hall is opened, a thousand people can be accommodated. The woods used in the Ark are those mentioned in the Bible, as are those in a wood sculpture atop the Ark which represents the word *chai*. On either side of the Ark are large and colorful stained-glass windows representing the parting of the Red Sea.

Calvary Community Church

What was to later become Calvary Community Church was founded in Thousand Oaks in the mid-1940s. That church, located on Skyline Drive, was struggling for existence by 1975. In an attempt to reverse the decline, a few dedicated families decided to search for a new pastor.

They succeeded in their search when they found the highly regarded minister of the First Missionary Church of Fort Wayne, Indiana—Pastor Larry DeWitt. After graduating from Wheaton College in Illinois, DeWitt had done his graduate studies at Fuller Theological Seminary in Pasadena where he was awarded both master's and doctorate degrees in divinity studies and ministry studies respectively. He also completed special studies at the Near East School of Archeological and Biblical Research in Jerusalem.

The church leaders also decided on an approach they would take to the community in order to reverse the decline—an emphasis on biblical teachings with relevant services and an abundance of programs to meet the emotional and spiritual needs of the area's residents. As a statement of this

new focus, the church began meeting in the Hungry Tiger Restaurant in Thousand Oaks. As the newly revised church prospered, a twenty-acre property was purchased at the intersection of the 101 and 23 Freeways. Plans and an architect's model were prepared for the future church but as the schedule for its construction was very long-range, the church rented a warehouse on Via Colinas in Westlake Village and moved in on March 23, 1980. The cavernous facility at first seemed much larger than required, but before long the congregation grew sufficiently to require a second Sunday service and eventually a Saturday night service was also inaugurated. Growth of the congregation also required more space for other church programs and periodically additional space for offices and meetings was rented in nearby buildings.

143

Calvary Community Church.

As the Calvary Community family reached four thousand, the rented facilities could no longer keep up with the growing number of church programs and services, so during the early and mid-1990s more consideration was given to building a new church on its twenty-acre property in Thousand Oaks. A search was also begun for other options—to lease or to buy a site large enough to meet the ultimate goal of serving up to twenty thousand people. That search resulted in the $8 million purchase of a thirty-six-acre site in Westlake Village on Via Rocas from the Eaton Corporation in December of 1997 and in the sale of the freeway intersection property to the City of Thousand Oaks on April 30, 1999, for about $2.5 million. As a major defense contractor, Eaton had provided highly classified electronic warfare systems and equipment to the U.S. military and some sections of the buildings still retain heavy missile-proof walls in former high-security areas.

The 310,000-square-foot building on the site was almost totally rebuilt at a cost of $11 million to provide 200,000 square feet of church service, meeting, office, and class-room space, as designed by Gensler Architects and built by the general contractor, Weseley-Thomas Enterprises, Inc., of Westlake Village.

The main sanctuary of the building referred to as the Celebration Center, seats twenty-eight hundred and is the largest auditorium between Los Angeles and San Francisco. It is equipped with five rear projection screens, some as large as twelve by sixteen feet, and has nearly one hundred speakers. The video system features computer graphics, text projection, and image magnification, all supported by separate video production, recording, and editing facilities.

The building also houses several meeting rooms with capacities up to five hundred people for banquets, weddings, and other large gatherings and nine secured early childhood center rooms for children from one month to five years. Additionally, there is an outdoor playground. A state-of-the-art personal pager system is available to each parent or guardian. The cafeteria and kitchen have a capacity to feed fifteen hundred people (which by reciprocal arrangement will also serve the Oaks Christian High School). All of the church administrative offices and conference rooms are accommodated within the main structure, along with a medical response room designed to handle on-site minor emergencies during church services and other large gatherings.

The church was sufficiently completed to permit holding the very first services in the new sanctuary on Sunday, April 3, 1999—Easter Sunday! The official dedication ceremonies attended by most of the forty-six-hundred-member congregation were held on Sunday, May 2, 1999, to celebrate the remarkable success—from a fading church twenty-four years earlier to one of the fastest growing, best funded churches in the country.

Westlake Lutheran Church

In 1970, the Division of Missions of the Lutheran Church decided a survey should be conducted to determine the viability of establishing a new church in Westlake Village. They selected Pastor Robert W. Lawson to conduct the study and to report his findings.

Prior to that assignment, Pastor Lawson had established Holy Trinity Lutheran Church in Thousand Oaks. He then served as its minister until 1967, when he became the director of admissions at California Lutheran College, a position he held until his new assignment in 1970.

An extensive series of calls throughout the community disclosed sufficient interest and the first services of the new congregation were held June 21, 1970, in the recreation building of the Dean Homes Community Center. By that time a significant ecumenical movement had been established in the community and the ministers of both the Westminster Presbyterian Church and the Westlake Methodist Church joined in the celebration. As with other churches in 1970, this new Lutheran congregation faced the challenge of space for its various endeavors. Since it was the start of summer, the key problem was space for the new Vacation Church School. The relationships established with other churches led to the solution—the new Lutheran Church joined with the Methodist and Presbyterian Churches and in a common effort the school was held at the First Neighborhood Community Center. Pastor Lawson's close working relationship with the Reverend Guy Morrison of the Methodist Church led to another unique event—on June 29, 1970, a joint celebration was held by their two congregations at the south shore of the lake—which at that time was all open space. In addition to the Vacation Church School, the two congregations shared in many other activities, among them Boy Scouts, youth groups, and boutiques.

In May of 1972 the Steering Committee of the church decided to apply to the Southwest Synod for official papers to become a formal church organization and to recognize the name as selected by the members of the congregation. They also sent a formal call to Pastor Lawson to become the pastor of record. The Southwest Synod helped the congregation with financial support and bought a 2.5-acre site at the southeast corner of Agoura and Lindero Canyon Roads from American-Hawaiian as a site for a future sanctuary. The church

Steering Committee continued its review of growth patterns and progress. With seven Lutheran Churches in the Conejo area and despite the growth of the congregation, it became doubtful that the membership would grow large enough in the foreseeable future to afford the cost of construction and to then support its own church building. Accordingly, the Steering Committee recommended the site be sold back to American-Hawaiian and requested the Synod keep open the option to buy another site as growth might indicate.

In the summer of 1972, the American-Hawaiian Information office at the southwest corner of Agoura and Lakeview Canyon Roads was lifted from its foundation and trailered west on Agoura Road to the southwest corner of Westlake Boulevard and Hampshire Road where it became the new home of the United Methodist Church of Westlake Village. While the Dean Homes facility had served well for Lutheran Church services, there was a serious lack of space for other church activities. Fortunately, the United Methodist congregation asked if Westlake Lutheran would consider joining them in their new location. A covenant agreement was drawn up and finally Westlake Lutheran had enough space available in one location for all its activities. The agreement was of advantage to the Methodist Church as well—rental payments as well as a $100,000 gift from the Lutherans to aid with their new building program. In 1984 the Church Council signed a new agreement extending the covenant agreement to the year 2000.

Because of space needs for their own activities, the United Methodist Church made the difficult decision in the spring of 1993 to close the Covenant relationship, to be effective in August 1994. The Lutheran congregation then made the move to another location at 2630 Townsgate Road. Continuous growth and the addition of both a director of family ministries and a youth director once again made it essential to seek a larger facility and a Capital Funds Campaign was established for that purpose.

Church of Jesus Christ of Latter-Day Saints

Westlake Village members at first attended a church on Moorpark Road in Thousand Oaks. In 1968, the Church authorities in Salt Lake City, Utah, recognized the need for a separate Westlake Village Chapel in the rapidly growing community and purchased a site at the northeast corner of LaVenta Drive and Watergate Road from American-Hawaiian Steamship Company through their agent, Bill Swan.

Otto J. Kover designed a church building and the plans for the new edifice were approved as compatible with Westlake Village standards by American-Hawaiian's building committee on April 5, 1972. On Saturday, December 2, 1972, groundbreaking ceremonies were held at the site, with the presiding Bishop Blaine H. Hall (then the presiding bishop of the Thousand Oaks Church) officiating. Many church members also attended the event as well as clergy from most of the Westlake Village churches.

referred to as the Cultural Hall which can be opened up to the Chapel to increase seating to eight hundred people, twenty-eight teaching stations, a modern kitchen with facilities to prepare food for up to several hundred, a kindergarten, a well-stocked library, and a separate room with the baptismal font.

After almost two years of construction, the new building was dedicated on February 27, 1974, by general church authorities from Salt Lake City and the new Bishop Ronald Call. Many other

Church of Jesus Christ of Latter Day Saints.

The Thousand Oaks Third Ward, the Agoura Ward, and the new Westlake Village Ward, all part of the Newbury Park Stake, designed the new church for use. Construction was started on the seventeen-thousand-square-foot sanctuary. It included the Chapel with a seating for over four hundred, a piano and imported organ, a large room

dignitaries from several Westlake Village churches, members of the new church and some members of the general public also attended the ceremony.

All funds to purchase the property and to construct the facility, including parking and landscaping, originated from tithing by church members from all over the world.

A van is kept on the church grounds to store clothing and other gifts from church members prior to their delivery to Deseret Industries, a Mormon Church organization, where they are refurbished if required, and then distributed to the needy.

Church of the Epiphany

A group of Westlake Village and Agoura residents began meeting in 1979 to investigate the possibility of founding an Episcopal Church to serve the two communities. By November, enough positive support had developed to warrant establishment of a steering committee. Guidance was provided by the Reverend Edward David Eagle, and words of encouragement were received from leaders of the Episcopal Churches in Thousand Oaks and Woodland Hills.

The original name for the new-church-to-be was St. Dunstan's Episcopal, but a few weeks later—with the first services of the new church scheduled for the start of the Epiphany season—the decision was made to change the name of the new church to Church of the Epiphany.

At noon on January 6, 1980, the steering committee scheduled a meeting in the sanctuary of the Westminster Presbyterian Church, with the purpose of determining how much interest there was in the communities for an Episcopal Church. The committee members expected the attendance of 30 to 40 people and were most pleasantly surprised when 134 people attended. At the services conducted by Reverend Eagle the supply of communion wafers ran out and had to be supplemented

Church of the Epiphany (Episcopalian).

with lemon cake–which was to have been served after the service!

The new church continued to hold services at Westminster Presbyterian Church until July 6, 1980, when Epiphany moved to the multipurpose room at White Oak Elementary School. With the move to a secular location, the church needed altar furniture and hangings. Member and Bishop's Warden John Detlie utilized his skills as a set designer to create a portable altar and member Harold Poett directed the building of a credence table and lectern. Led by members Rebecca Mills and Mary Rummell, the women of the church designed and created altar frontal and seasonal hangings.

The year 1980 also saw the start of fundraising for a new sanctuary. Among those efforts was a bus trip to Lompoc to Harold Poett's ranch where the Mission Guild served a luncheon and the group learned the history of the ranch, one of many granted to Poett's great-great-grandfather, Captain Jose Antonio Julian de la Guerra y Noriega. The effort toward obtaining a site for a new church was furthered when Kris Carraway-Bowman, then with American-Hawaiian Land Company, advised of a property in Oak Park that had been specifically designated as a church site. The property, then accessible only by Jeep or on foot, was priced at $400,000. When Bishop Rusack of the Episcopal Diocese

of Los Angeles saw the property, he too was impressed with its beauty. Subsequently, the Diocese bought the property in March of 1987 with the proviso that the Epiphany congregation would raise $100,000 toward the purchase. The hilly property north of Kanan Road was in an area then known as Sutton Valley and as the area developed a new street was built providing access to the site and named Churchwood Drive.

A Building Committee headed by Kris Carraway-Bowman and others was formed to seek out the type of church architecture desired by the congregation. A parish-wide survey had established very definitely that the choice was for a sanctuary that "looked like a traditional Episcopal Church, not a Spanish style and it must have a steeple." The dedicated members of the committee spent many long weekend hours touring Southern California in search of a church design that would meet those requirements and posted photographs of churches they had visited in the lobby for review by church members after Sunday services. Finally, a church in Los Olivos was located that seemed to meet most requirements. Gary Heathcote, the architect retained by the church, was taken to see and evaluate the Los Olivos Church.

Unlike the Westlake Village area, there were some regions in Southern

California that were losing population. Sunland-Tujunga was one such location, and leaders of Epiphany had learned that the Church of the Ascension located there was about to be deconsecrated. Members of the Epiphany congregation visited the Ascension Church, attended services there and were gifted with a baptismal font, altar silver, a processional cross and torches, linen vestments, and twenty-four stained-glass windows depicting the life of Christ. These windows had been imported from Europe about one hundred years prior and are now incorporated into the windows as designed for the new Church of the Epiphany. Leaders of the Epiphany Church investigated the possibility of dismantling the Ascension Church and moving it to the Epiphany site. The project was abandoned after extensive studies showed that structural concerns, travel route problems, and costs made it impractical.

The year 1993 saw the establishment of a Bishop's Committee, headed by Penny Yarrow and Jim McGlothlin, to raise the funds for design and construction of the new church. The highly successful drive permitted the start of work only six months later and soon the plans of architect Gary Heathcote started to take form under the guidance of general contractor Lee Woodward. Walter Judson worked in concert with Woodward on the design details of the beautiful interior, including the European stained-glass windows.

The Church of the Epiphany was completed in November of 1984 and was consecrated by Bishop Borsch of the Episcopal Diocese of Los Angeles on January 7, 1985–Epiphany Sunday!

Westminster Presbyterian Church

In 1968 the New Church Development Committee of the Synod of Southern California invited the Reverend Robert C. Bos to work as the organizing pastor in establishing a church in the new community of Westlake Village. At the time the only residents were those in First Neighborhood and starting March 1, the Reverend Bos went door-to-door introducing himself and determining the interest in establishing a Presbyterian Church in the community.

His success was confirmed by the first service held on Palm Sunday at the First Neighborhood Community Center. Training for a church school staff was started and classes began six weeks later. In September, church services were moved to the recently completed White Oak Elementary School.

On November 10, 1968, the Presbytery of San Fernando officially organized the congregation with 161 members of 77 families, and Reverend Bos was called to be the church's first pastor.

After the church was officially organized, the first services were held on November 18, 1968, again at White Oak Elementary where they continued to be held until they started to worship at the First Neighborhood Community Center. On October 8, 1970, the origination of the church's Women's Guild took place.

Three and one-half acres of land had been purchased in 1966 at the corner of Lakeview Canyon and Watergate Roads by the Synod of San Fernando and, on May 24, 1970, ground was broken for a new church edifice. The new building, consisting of the sanctuary, classrooms, multipurpose room, and offices, as designed by Fisher and Wilde, saw the first services on May 23, 1971. The official dedication was held on June 6, 1971, with Reverend Arthur Bailey,

director of new church development of the Synod of Southern California, assisting in the ceremonies. It was noted at the time as being the first church edifice to be built in Westlake Village.

On August 13, 1971, the last session of the vacation church school was held—a very successful ecumenical program conducted by the Presbyterian, Methodist, and Lutheran faiths. A prayer service evidenced other examples of ecumenicism at Covenant House, attended by clergy and members of the Presbyterian, Lutheran, Catholic, and Methodist Churches. Also, there was a Thanksgiving Eve service held on November 22, 1972, at St. Jude's Catholic Church, attended by parishioners and clergy from the United Methodist, Westlake Lutheran, West-

151

Westminster Presbyterian Church.

minster Presbyterian, and Temple Adat Elohim houses of worship. Music was provided by the Ecumenical Choir.

On June 20, 1976, in recognition of the Bicentennial year, the Westminster congregation held services at Old North Church at Forest Lawn Memorial Park in Hollywood Hills. The Church is a replica of the famous Old North Church in Boston. Reverend Bos delivered a modified form of the liturgy used two hundred years earlier and he and many members of the congregation wore costumes of the late 1770s.

On September 10, 1986, the Westlake Village City Council approved an addition of 13,560 square feet to the existing structure. The plans included enlargement of the existing sanctuary to seat over 400, a music rehearsal room, the construction of a separate fellowship hall to seat 350, kitchen facilities, and enlargement of the administration wing.

In 1996, the church inaugurated a very unusual and special annual Christmas event: the Bethlehem Experience. For three nights a drive-through pageant provides the public an opportunity to see life as it was at the time of the birth of Christ. Over one hundred members of the Westminster Church dress in costumes, portraying merchants, shepherds, tax collectors, priests, scribes, and homeless nomads. At the entrance, motorists pass through the gates of Bethlehem guarded by

Roman sentries, and then past a synagogue, traveler's camp, housewives shopping at merchants' stalls, and of course, a nativity scene. In the three evenings it is open, up to thirty-five hundred cars pass through to witness this event.

March 29, 1987, saw the ground-breaking for the new construction, with Reverend Robert Bos and many members wielding shovels to mark the occasion.

On Sunday, January 10, 1988, dedication ceremonies were held for the new addition with Reverend Dr. Robert C. Bos officiating. Participating guests included Reverend Frederick Beebe of the Synod of Southern California and Hawaii, and Reverend Joreen Jarell, executive presbyter of the Presbytery of San Fernando.

In September 1989, Reverend Dr. Bos traveled to China in the company of astronaut James Irwin (who drove the lunar rover on the moon in 1971) and eighty-five other Americans. They were allowed to visit Tiananmen Square, the scene of the pro-democracy riots on June 3-4, even though it was still closed to the Chinese. Their travels included the Great Wall, the Nanking Theological Seminary, and a visit with Bishop Ting, the president of the China Council of Churches.

As the Westminster Church prospered and the congregation increased, the need for more space grew year by year. After detail evaluations and design reviews, plans for major additions were submitted to the city and were approved on October 25, 2000. The program calls for the removal of the present administrative wing facing Watergate and replacing it with a two-story structure, building an alcove balcony in the sanctuary, adding a second story to the Fellowship Hall, and constructing a new two-story building along Lakeview Canyon Road with the preschool on the first floor and the Sunday school on the second. Additionally, a bell tower will be built in the atrium area.

United Methodist Church of Westlake Village

In response to the growing need for a Methodist Church in Westlake Village, Dr. Richard Cain of the Methodist Conference arranged for the purchase of three acres of land at the southwest corner of Westlake Boulevard and Hampshire Road at a cost of $150,000. A gift of $50,000 from the Southern California–Arizona Conference helped with the purchase, as did a 1 percent loan. In 1967 a sign was placed on the property "The Future Home of the Methodist Church."

In August of 1969, Reverend Guy Morrison was assigned by the Department of New Church Development of the United Methodist Board of Missions in New York to start a new church in the area and to be its first minister. As with leaders of other faiths, Reverend Morrison rang doorbells throughout the Westlake community to raise interest in the new venture.

After only two and one-half weeks of that effort, the first services were held at the First Neighborhood Community Center on September 14, 1969. Bishop Gerald B. Kennedy conducted services and thirty families were received as members of the new church. In fifteen months the congregation had grown to over two hundred, and continued to meet in the main room at First Neighborhood every Sunday at 11:00 a.m., while the Sunday school met at 10:00 a.m. in partitioned spaces. Several church groups met at the Village Homes clubhouse, where the choir rehearsed. Some other groups met at the homes of Reverend Morrison and several members. It came to Reverend Morrison's attention that Security Pacific Bank had acquired the property at the southwest corner of Lakeview Canyon and Agoura Roads, and intended to demolish the American-Hawaiian Information Center located on it. On October 22, 1970, Security Pacific agreed to donate the buildings if the church would pay the cost of moving them and gave the church until January 1, 1971, to complete the job.

United Methodist Church
of Westlake Village.
(Courtesy Carol Ames,
photographer)

In December, the 160 tons of buildings were separated from their foundations and moved west on Agoura Road. Because they had been built to Los Angeles County codes and were to be installed to Ventura County standards, considerable work had to be accomplished. The buildings were temporarily stored at the IBM building site on Townsgate Road where they survived the 1971 earthquake. Peter Candreva, a church member, handled design work for the structures. Another church member, Wayne Fogelsong, was selected as the contractor to prepare the site and to modify and erect the buildings. The formal groundbreaking

ceremony was held on Sunday, January 17, 1971, and a target date of Easter Sunday in March was set for the official opening. But construction delays and code compliance caused the date to be put off until Mother's Day, Sunday May 9, 1971, when 284 charter members joined in the celebration. In January 1972, a service of consecration was held, with Bishop Gerald Kennedy presiding.

During this period, a recommendation was made to liquidate the Agoura Methodist Church, to merge it with the Westlake Church, and to use the resulting funds to assist the Westlake facility. The superintendent of the fifty-two Methodist Churches comprising the

Santa Barbara District drew up the necessary paperwork. The Agoura Church site was then sold to the Agoura Valley Baptist Chapel.

As elsewhere noted, Pastor Robert Lawson of the Westlake Lutheran Church and Reverend Guy Morrison had become close friends and had worked closely together on a number of efforts. When arrangements were concluded not only for Lutheran services to be held at the new facility, but for Friday night services of Temple Adat Elohim as well, it was named Covenant House.

On July 5, 1973, construction of a new Christian Education building was started, again designed by Peter Candreva. It was completed on February 8, 1976, and named Alton Hall after an early church benefactor. The congregation laid all the roof tiles over a fourteen-month period and the last cap tile, which had been obtained from the San Luis Obispo Mission, was signed by all the children who attended that first service.

As the church prospered, it became evident that the refurbished American-Hawaiian Information Center buildings could no longer serve its needs. In 1977, a Building Study Committee was formed to establish the long-range needs of the church, the types of buildings required, and the costs and means of fundraising. Under the direction of church member

Lucy Hanley, years of intensive and successful effort followed and a new sanctuary and a multiplicity of other service rooms and offices, designed by William Overpeck and Larry Gilman, were constructed by R. Rushio at a cost of $1.2 million.

A community celebration was held on May 5, 1985, by both the Methodist and Lutheran congregations to mark the opening of the new sanctuary and Sunday school with its play yard. Consecration Services followed on June 30, 1985, with Methodist Bishop Jack Tuell and Lutheran Bishop Stanley Olsen presiding. Groundbreaking for a new Youth Building was held on July 26, 1986, and the structure was completed and opened the following year.

Volunteerism is a way of life in the Westlake Village community. Local chapters of the American Heart Association, the Cancer Foundation, the Wellness Community, Senior Concerns, and many, many other organizations find strong support from the residents of Westlake Village. Just a few of the earliest groups are highlighted here, but their dedicated volunteers are typical of the community as a whole.

The Westlake Women's Club

In early 1968, about fifty women of the immediate area met at the First Neighborhood Community Center to discuss the founding of a women's group. Soon thereafter about twenty-five of the women organized a social club with Ann Homel as its first president. In 1971, the club, with then president Elizabeth Thompson, became affiliated with the California Federation of Women's Clubs—and changed its basic purpose from social to philanthropic.

The major fundraising event for the club in recent years has been a spring fashion show and luncheon at the Hyatt Westlake Hotel. It is well attended and many elegant gift baskets and other valuable items are raffled off. A number of these prizes are donated by local businesses. The net income from this event comprises the largest part of the philanthropic funds distributed by the club.

As a member of the California Federation, the Westlake Village Women's Club distributes 80 percent of the proceeds to local charities within the Conejo Valley, with the remaining 20 percent held in reserve to support the district, state, and nationally approved projects. Canine Companions, the March of Dimes, and the California Federation Art Fund are some of the traditional programs supported by the club.

Recipients of local funding range from the Agoura Animal Shelter through Conejo Valley Senior Concerns and Hospice of the Conejo to Zonta Special Kid's Day. The largest contributions are for scholarships awarded to local youth.

Operating funds for the club are raised at an annual luncheon and tea-modeling, titled Holiday Fantasy, held at one of the country clubs in the area—with the exception of membership dues, all other club income goes to the philanthropies.

The club has been the recipient of many awards—including one from then U.S. Senator Hayakawa as the outstanding service club in California.

The club has also been honored three times by the Westlake Village Chamber of Commerce as the area's outstanding service club. For their outstanding efforts in landscaping the 101 Freeway–Lindero Canyon Road interchange, they were honored with a "Keep America Beautiful" National Award.

After more than thirty years of service to the community, the club is more active than ever. With over eighty-five members involved in the arts, education, home life, public affairs, and many other areas, the club is a strong and vital part of the community.

Meals on Wheels

The Westlake Village Meals on Wheels program was organized in 1982 and started with fundraising in early 1983. A commitment was received from Westlake Community Hospital to provide meal preparation services. By mid-February, with major donations from the Methodist Men of Thousand Oaks and the Westlake Rotary Club, sufficient funding was available to start the program. Similar to other Meals on Wheels programs, it was designed for the elderly and convalescents without adequate transportation.

Recipients, if financially able, were requested to pay five dollars a day for one hot meal at lunch and one cold meal at dinner, to be delivered to their homes, Monday through Friday. With funding in hand and volunteer delivery drivers lined up, the service started on March 28, 1983, with seven "customers."

The "prime movers" for this program were Kris Carraway and Bonnie Klove (see Appendix F for a list of the original officers and directors). The program continued after the closure of the Westlake Hospital, with meals prepared by several commercial establishments. More recently, State Farm Insurance Company on Agoura Road has been preparing the meals at their facility.

The program is active and growing. The organization provides about three hundred meals each month to Westlake Village residents on both sides of the county line, as well as in Agoura and Oak Park, with occasional requests from Calabasas. Seventeen volunteer drivers are now active in delivering these meals, two of whom are original volunteers from 1983.

It is of particular interest to note that community support has enabled the Meals on Wheels organization to keep the cost to the recipients at only six dollars a day, up from five dollars a day in 1982!

Disaster Response Team

The city issued a call in 1994 for volunteers to revise the city's Disaster Preparedness booklet. Ten citizens were appointed to an Emergency Preparedness/ Disaster Response Committee, which within months completed the assigned task. In March of 1995, the City of Westlake Village Disaster Response Team (DRT) was formed, and twelve of its members were appointed as a committee to formulate a constitution and by-laws for this new organization. (Appendix E)

Initially, thirty-five members of the community successfully completed the basic training courses designed to provide them with the skills necessary to perform their assigned functions in the event of a disaster. With the expansion of its capabilities, the DRT operates with a number of specialty teams, each trained in detail to perform its basic function:

Disaster Response

Urban Search and Rescue

Medical

Incident Command

Disaster Support

Communications

Most members of the DRT are trained—and retrained quarterly—to work on all or most of these teams. The Medical group is trained not only in Cardio-Pulmonary Resuscitation (CPR), but also in the use of the state-of-the-art Automatic External Defibrillator (AED).

These dedicated teams are always in a state of readiness, twenty-four hours a day, 365 days a year. Each member is trained and equipped to respond in sixty minutes or less to any disaster in the area, such as earthquakes, wild fires, civil unrest, flooding, mudslides, toxic chemical release, aircraft crashes, missing or lost citizens, or any other situations that might negatively affect residents of the city. They are equipped and trained to perform their duties for up to seventy-two hours, independent of outside aid, and are also prepared and trained to work with or under the direction of county, state, or federal agencies in such disasters.

The city is most fortunate in having this large group of citizens who have taken—and continue to take—much of their time in training and practice to insure that any disasters occurring within the city are met with an early and prompt response. Their charter is to operate during such disasters and to provide coordinated relief services and necessary first aid, while staying in communication with City Hall and other designated authorities.

Disaster Response Team. Left to right: Debby Gustafson, Jeff Friedman, Irmgard Wood, Ron Elliot, Margie Price, and Larry Svoboda.

The DRT has jurisdiction over a major inventory of disaster response supplies and equipment—numbering in the thousands of individual items and ranging from heavy duty tools to medical supplies to portable radios, power generators, floodlights, and protective clothing. Members of the DRT are constantly in training with this equipment to insure their missions can be carried out with dispatch.

The DRT must be activated officially in order to perform its duties—the City Council, the Sheriff's Department, or the Fire Department can initiate the order for activation. Only in the event of a disaster so extreme that all normal means of communication are compromised can the DRT self-activate.

In addition to its disaster mission, the DRT is also used to provide first aid, communication and safety services at community occasions—park concerts, parades, races, and holiday events. The group also publishes a newsletter covering information on recent and upcoming activities and training sessions.

Westlake Community Hospital Auxiliary

In February of 1972, a group of women, known as the volunteer Westlake Village Guild at the Los Robles Hospital in Thousand Oaks, decided to organize a similar group to serve the new Westlake Community Hospital. Under their president, Shirley Bourland, the group held a membership drive luncheon in February of 1972, almost a year before the hospital opened. Despite the unfinished surroundings, the sack lunches and leaky plastic champagne glasses, the event was a success with eighty-seven women joining the group.

In June, the first officers of the new organization were installed—Marian Carey as president, CoCo Strang as vice-president, Maria Popodopolous as secretary, and Jerry Harkness as treasurer. The group held its first fundraiser, a "Fiesta," at the Landing in September, which raised almost $5,000. Much of the money was spent in decorating the hospital's pediatrics ward with appropriate wallpaper, Disney cartoon character plaques, and many toys, as well as 120 stuffed pillow ducks made by the auxiliary members.

The incorporation papers for the Auxiliary were filed on November 3, 1972, signed by three directors: Brendon R. Fonner, Gail Harrington, and Shirley Roberts. The documents were signed by then Secretary of State Edmond G. Brown on November 11. Finally, the hospital had its official dedication and grand opening on December 8, 1972, and the Auxiliary—aided by the Candy Stripers—conducted tours of the facility.

The first patients were admitted to the new hospital on December 18, 1972, and the next day the very first baby was born. To mark the occasion, both child and mother were presented with gifts from the Auxiliary.

The Auxiliary opened the Alcove on January 4, 1973, and for many years it was a most welcome source for patient gifts, snacks, and personal goods. Profits from that venture were always distributed to local charities.

The Auxiliary thrived and provided much appreciated services to the patients and to the hospital for many years, and through several changes in its ownership from Safecare Company (the original group of doctors) through Universal Health Services and Columbia HCA to Salick Specialty Enterprises. When the Salick organization closed the facility on July 17, 1987, the Auxiliary's services to the hospital came to an end.

Many of the members found other volunteer activities with a number of public service agencies in the area. Others joined the Los Robles Regional Medical Center Auxiliary—and many have stayed together as a social group, sharing the pleasant recollections of their days of service at Westlake Community Hospital.

Volunteers in Policing (V.I.P.)

Inaugurated in 2002, this group of local citizens is trained by the Sheriff's Department to act as the eyes and ears of the department as they patrol the city.

At present, patrolling is conducted during daytime hours using a city-owned and marked vehicle, with two volunteers in two to three hour shifts.

Working in teams, these volunteers watch for unusual situations, talk to children on the streets during school hours, check on homes when notified the occupants are on vacation, patrol store parking lots (where most car break-ins occur), and assist deputies at public events. While they are not tactically involved in police actions such as apprehension and arrest, it is agreed that they provide the best type of law enforcement by their visible presence in the community.

These volunteers have all completed a training course provided by the Sheriff's Department, which included use of radios through which they can readily communicate with the Lost Hills Sheriff's Station. These volunteers also attend ongoing training classes.

While they do not carry weapons or make arrests, they wear uniforms while on patrol in the marked car. These volunteers provide their own uniform jackets with identifying sleeve patches.

It is interesting to note that three members of one family are counted among the ten volunteers. (Appendix L)

Many other amenities in Westlake Village have also contributed to the lifestyle enjoyed in this community. Whether they are the product of the initial planning or later controlled development, each became an essential part of the whole, has its own history and has made its own contribution in turning raw ranch land into one of the most livable communities in the country.

Only a few really controversial issues have needed resolution by City Councils over the years. In each instance, as noted here, they were resolved equitably to the satisfaction of most of our residents.

First Neighborhood

In recognition of the need for special amenities to attract potential homebuyers out to the "City in the Country," American-Hawaiian invested heavily in a number of then unusual features for the initial development—first called "The Park," but soon changed to "First Neighborhood."

First Neighborhood model homes, 1966: Colony Park (left) and Mayfair (right).

In addition to building a Community Center and a gated swimming pool at cost of over $1 million, American-Hawaiian also provided the roof for the White Oak Elementary School to insure compatibility with nearby residences. A small shopping center with a bank, mini-market, and other shops was built near the Community Center. The adjacent Reyes (later Berniece Bennett) Park was built and donated to Los Angeles County. The residential areas were laid out so that most of the 666 homes were on cul-de-sacs, many of which led to the one and one-third miles of landscaped greenbelts which permitted elementary school children to walk to school without crossing a street.

All the cul-de-sacs were laid out to connect with four "collector" streets, which connected to five "gates" streets (Greengate, Watergate, etc.) which in turn led to the main thoroughfares—Agoura, Lindero Canyon, and Lakeview Canyon Roads. The costs of providing the infrastructure (power, water, sewers, etc.) were considerably higher for the cul-de-sac pattern than for the usual "through street" design.

Two builders, Shattuck-McCone and Lee-Lasky, partnered with American-Hawaiian on a 40–60 percent basis and in mid-1966 started construction on the two developments, named Mayfair Homes and Colony Park respectively. Ultimately, 397 Mayfair homes

First Neighborhood Shopping Center, circa 1967.

and 269 of the zero-lot-line construction homes in Colony Park were built. Both builders started sales operations in a temporary structure north of the 101 Highway, and later moved to their model home sites, Lee-Lasky on Coolhaven Court and Shattuck-McCone on Allenby Court. American-Hawaiian built an Information Center at the southwest corner of Agoura and Lakeview Canyon Roads. It featured a large relief map of the entire Westlake Village development as then planned, showing the two golf courses, all the various home developments—including two high-rise buildings at the west end of the lake! When the Information Center was no longer needed it was detached from its foundations and in December 1970 was trailered west on Agoura Road across the county line where it was to become the first sanctuary of the Methodist Church.

The first residents of First Neighborhood—and thus of Westlake Village—were members of the Johnson family. (Jim Johnson was then the chief financial officer of American-Hawaiian.) When they moved into their new home at the east end of Foxmoor Court next to the greenbelt, no utilities had as yet been connected—telephone, gas, or water—so they had to do with a water truck to provide sanitary service.

As with all subsequent Westlake Village residential areas, all First Neighborhood homeowners were, and still are, bound by contract to observe certain rules, known as Covenants, Conditions and Restrictions (the C.C.& Rs). The elected Boards of Directors of the eighteen homeowner associations (excepting The Ridge) manage those rules for each neighborhood. They have served the community well over the years, and have helped to maintain the ambiance for which Westlake Village is nationally recognized.

Mayfair Homes price list, 1966.

163

WESTLAKE VILLAGE

MAYFAIR SERIES

TRACT 25404

PAYMENT SCHEDULE

Effective Date 8/22/66

Plan	Sales Price	10% Min. Down Pmt.	1st T.D. 6-1/2% 30 years	Monthly Payment	2nd T.D. 6-1/2% 24 years	Monthly Payment	Total Monthly Pmt.
130	$30,800	$3,100	$23,100	$147.00	$4,600	$32.00	$179.00
140	$30,800	$3,100	$23,100	$147.00	$4,600	$32.00	$179.00
190-2	$31,875	$3,190	$23,900	$152.00	$4,785	$33.00	$185.00
190-3	$32,400	$3,240	$24,300	$154.00	$4,860	$34.00	$188.00
200	$33,900	$3,400	$25,400	$161.00	$5,100	$35.00	$196.00
210-2	$34,875	$3,490	$26,100	$166.00	$5,285	$37.00	$203.00
210-3	$35,425	$3,545	$26,500	$168.00	$5,380	$37.00	$205.00
220	$35,875	$3,590	$26,900	$171.00	$5,385	$37.00	$208.00

The Lake

As noted, the original Bechtel study for the Albertson Ranch did not include a lake. Early considerations by American-Hawaiian on handling Triunfo Creek included a concrete channel similar to that of some parts of the Los Angeles River,

Triunfo Creek prior to dam construction.

Clearing the dam site.

or a rock "rip-rap" channel with sloping sides. Neither of those options were found to adequately represent the "City in the Country" concept. Further studies showed that desirable and attractive waterfront properties could be generated by the construction of a lake. After presenting a study on the lake proposal to D. K. Ludwig, he approved the plan. Accordingly, McIntire and Quiros, an engineering company, was retained to design the facility. Pascal and Ludwig Engineering Company started construction in 1966. The first activity involved building the seven-hundred-foot-long, three-story-high concrete gravity dam to impound water from local springs and runoff from Lake Sherwood and Hidden Valley. The dam, with release gates to insure water flow to downstream facilities, used 22,500 cubic yards of concrete (enough for seventeen miles of four-lane highway). The unique shoreline, designed by Julian George, was composed of natural soil and concrete, sculpted with high-pressure water hoses. The entire lake project was completed in 1969 at a cost of $3.5 million.

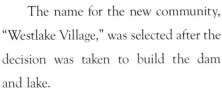

A highly unique feature was the construction of Westlake Island, partially built up with materials from the lake site. Because the island stretches across the county line, both Los Angeles and Ventura Counties required a bridge access. After negotiations, American-Hawaiian received approval to build only one bridge—right on the county line—and designed to meet the differing standards of the two counties. To commemorate that location, American-Hawaiian named the street that crosses the bridge "LaVenta" after the two counties. As a gated and guarded community, Westlake Island maintains its own streets and other amenities through its homeowner association.

The name for the new community, "Westlake Village," was selected after the decision was taken to build the dam and lake.

Upon its completion, the nine-mile shoreline, 150-acre lake, had an average depth of ten feet, and was stocked with three thousand large-mouth bass and three thousand blue channel catfish. As a man-made lake, its ecology was a matter of major concern and upon completion, the University of California at Riverside was retained to provide scientific advice. It was also noted the terrain is such that the area of runoff to the lake exceeds twenty-eight square miles.

Left: The dam. (Courtesy Lussier Photography)

165

Westlake Island and lake under construction, circa 1968.

Right: The lake.

Far right: Sailing regatta on Westlake Lake.

Lake Management Offices. (Courtesy Lussier Photography)

A total of thirteen hundred homes front on or have ready access to the lake, many of whose residents own electric or sailboats for recreational sailing or fishing. Each home is assessed an annual fee used for maintenance of the lake, dam, and other facilities. The Westlake Lake Management Association, whose thirty-three-member Board is comprised of representatives from each lake-front homeowner association manages maintenance of the lake.

A major feature of the lake is the Westlake Yacht Club with its clubhouse and docking facilities near the dam. The club provides many social events for its members and their guests, and sponsors sailing classes and regattas for its youthful members.

Ownership of the Westlake Lake and its facilities was transferred to the lakeside homeowners in January 1974, in accord with prior agreements with the partnership of American-Hawaiian and Prudential.

The Westlake Yacht Club

Sailing enthusiasts banded together in 1969 to incorporate the Westlake Yacht Club. The club rented the building then known as the Boat House, which had been used as the boat salesroom at The Landing. After some renovation, the club purchased the building in 1974. By 1996 the building loan was retired, and a symbolic mortgage burning was held. The clubhouse is used regularly for members' social events and meetings, and upon occasion is rented to other individuals or organizations.

In 1971 the club became a member of the Southern California Yachting Association (SCYA), the United States Sailing Association, and the United States Yacht Racing Union. The club achieved SCYA Senior Member status in 1983—the highest level of membership in the organization—and is the only Inland Yacht Club to attain that status. The club was further honored by SCYA as Yacht Club of the Year for the 1998 sailing season, in competition with the largest yacht clubs in Southern California.

Sailing near island homes on Westlake Lake. (Courtesy Lussier Photography)

Island Homes. (Courtesy Lussier Photography)

The club operates a very heavy regatta program and is involved in youth and community activities. An outstanding event is the annual Sail-A-Thon in which teams race from 11 a.m. to 9 p.m. over a course handicapped to insure that different classes of boats sail the same distance. Over the years a classic car show has been added to the all-day event generating even more interest in the race.

The club sponsors a Junior Sailing program which has its own officers, as well as sponsoring sailing teams at Agoura, Westlake, and Chaminade High Schools in the West Coast Inter-Scholastic Sailing Association. An international organization of past yacht club commodores awards a college scholarship to an outstanding graduate member of the club's Junior Sailing program.

A highlight in the club's history occurred in 1998 when a former member of the Junior Sailing program, Allison Jolly, won a gold medal in sailing at the Olympic games in Seoul, South Korea—the first time sailing was recognized in Olympic competition.

Activities of the Yacht Club are directed by three top officers: the commodore, vice commodore, and rear commodore. Each year a new rear commodore is elected by the club membership, and the current rear commodore and vice commodore move up to the next position.

Westlake Yacht Club. (Courtesy Lussier Photography)

Westlake Island

Once the Island and the LaVenta Bridge were completed and prior to start of residential construction, American-Hawaiian provided fireworks on the Fourth of July for Westlake residents. Groups gathered to watch the show on empty residential sites up on the hillside in what was to become Parkwood Estates.

Monarch Construction Company started construction of Island homes in 1968. Harold Levitt, A.I.A., designed these homes. There were seven models to choose from, up to thirty-one hundred square feet, both single and two-story. Prices ranged up from $49,950. The Island has many custom-

built homes, one of the first of which was built on a double lot for David Stockton, then the golf professional at the Westlake Golf Course.

Most of the homes have their own docks to accommodate the electric boats and sailboats so popular with Island residents. There are also a few kayaks, single sculls, and pedal boats for those desiring exercise. Fishing is also a popular pastime, with bass, catfish, and crappies being taken from favorite spots. All fish caught must be returned, no live bait can be used, and all hooks must be barbless.

The 313 families who enjoy the Island living are protected by twenty-four-hour guards on duty at the single gated entrance to the Island at the mainland end of LaVenta Drive. As noted elsewhere, the bridge that gives access to the Island is built on the county line, one-half in Los Angeles County and the other in Ventura County which made for some interesting bureaucratic problem solving.

Even though the county line divides the Island, police and fire services are readily available from the two counties. However, as a private and gated community, the homeowner association provides other services such as street lighting, parkway landscaping, and street sweeping.

White Oak Elementary School

When American-Hawaiian laid out First Neighborhood, they set aside 8.7 net acres for a school, offered to sell the site to the Las Virgenes Unified School District and named the street fronting the property "Village School Road."

The district recorded escrow on the acreage on October 19, 1966, at a purchase price of $196,797 showing the address as "School Site–Albertson Ranch." To accommodate the rapidly growing population in the area the district moved classroom trailers onto the adjacent Reyes Adobe Park for the many kindergarten through grade five students.

Construction contracts totaling $765,732 were awarded to K. & F. Construction Company and Lowan Construction Company for the sixteen classrooms, 33,297 total square feet of buildings. The project was completed in the spring of 1968 and the students proudly marched across the field during spring break—from the trailers to the beautiful and modern new facility—each carrying a tote tray with all his or her personal school supplies.

Over the years, the White Oak School student body population has ranged up and down. At a low point in the early 1980s with a count of not much over two hundred students, the district considered closing the facility for economic reasons. By transferring students from another grade school, and with an influx of children from the Three Springs housing development, that action was canceled, much to the relief of local parents.

Ultimately, with occasional student counts of over seven hundred, the district funded an expansion of an eight-thousand-square-foot addition at a cost of $2.5 million. A major feature is a multi-purpose room equipped with state-of-the-art communications.

Since its opening in 1968, White Oak Elementary has always been a highly rated and admired school, especially during the years it received national recognition at ceremonies in Washington, D.C.

White Oak
Elementary School.

The Hospital

In early 1972, a group of local doctors obtained funding support and had a small hospital built near the intersection of Lakeview Canyon and Agoura Roads. The new full-service facility, named Westlake Community Hospital, was dedicated on Saturday, December 9, of that year. In attendance were Robert Fuller of the NBC series "Emergency," Los Angeles County Supervisor Baxter Ward, Dr. Jerry Ratzan, chairman of the hospital's Board of Directors and many other notables. At the time of its opening, the hospital was licensed for 110 beds and included an emergency room, birthing center, surgery, intensive care unit, plus pediatric and outpatient areas.

In June of 1981, the hospital was purchased from the doctor-owners by Universal Health Care of King of Prussia, Pennsylvania, and was later renamed Westlake Medical Center. The hospital census (number of bed patients) slowly decreased, and the license was reduced from 110 to 75 beds. For a brief period a small area of the facility was converted to psychiatric care. In 1994, about one-quarter of the hospital area was leased to Salick Healthcare for oncology treatment. The agreement included an option for Salick to purchase the entire facility for certain limited hospital services.

The Universal organization was approached by a larger hospital chain,

Westlake Community Hospital.

Columbia HCA (which owned the Los Robles Hospital in Thousand Oaks) about an exchange of hospital facilities—Columbia's Aiken, South Carolina hospital for Universal's Dallas, Texas Family Hospital, plus a smaller facility to balance the deal—which turned out to be the Westlake Medical Center. The exchange was finalized on July 7, 1995. Columbia then signed a new lease with Salick for continuation of cancer treatment in the hospital, again with an option to buy the whole facility for the limited uses, the same as previously agreed with Universal. Within a year, Salick exercised that option, took possession and renamed it Salick Specialty Hospital. However, since Salick did not intend to operate an emergency room, it was closed just prior to the transfer of ownership.

Shortly after the acquisition, Salick sued Columbia in Federal Court over the usage restrictions imposed by their contractual agreement. After operating it as a specialty hospital for about a year, Salick closed the facility on July 31, 1997. As the lawsuit progressed, a British pharma-

171

ceutical company, Zeneca, Ltd., which had previously purchased 50 percent of all Salick Healthcare's operations in the United States and Great Britain, in turn exercised an option it held to buy the balance of the Salick holdings. With that purchase, Zeneca inherited the Salick lawsuit and the closed Westlake Hospital building. After protracted negotiations, Zeneca and Columbia negotiated a settlement—the lawsuit was dropped and ownership of the closed hospital building was returned to Columbia. After remaining closed for almost two years, the building was partially refurbished and reopened December 19, 1999, as an Urgent Care facility with limited hours. Several rehabilitation operations and the Los Robles business offices were also relocated to the site.

Both prior to and after the closure, the Westlake Village City Council repeatedly expressed its concerns about possible effects the closure might have on local health care. In June 1998 the Council sent letters to twelve of the largest national hospital organizations in an attempt to develop interest in building a hospital in the area. All replies received were negative, citing economic factors.

In September 1999, protracted discussions were held with Los Angeles County Supervisor Zev Yaroslavsky and several of his deputies in an attempt to obtain a small part of the county's tobacco settlement funds as seed money to fund a land purchase to make a deal more attractive to a hospital company. That effort was unsuccessful. Nevertheless, an extensive study was instituted by the county on hospital needs for this area. The county's chief administrative officer issued a ten-page report with over fifty pages of supporting data on November 1, 1999, detailing the reasons for refusal. Some time later, the five-city local Council of Governments (COG) declined to consider the issue as a priority.

After the Westlake Medical Center was closed in July 1996 it became necessary for the Los Angeles County Fire Department's Emergency Medical Services to transport patients, when required, to Los Robles Regional Medical Center. However, shortly after the Westlake facility closed, the county assigned a second EMS unit to the area which, according to county reports, resulted in a 17 percent quicker response time by paramedics than prior to the Westlake Hospital closure.

In early 1997, an Ad Hoc Committee of two City Council members was appointed to meet with any groups which expressed an interest in establishing a local hospital, and to review any data that reportedly indicated the need. After several years without appreciable results, the committee was disbanded by the City Council early in 2000.

The Reservoir

Early in 1970, the Las Virgenes Municipal Water District recognized the future need for more backup water storage to serve the expanding Westlake Village area. Negotiations with American-Hawaiian resulted in the donation of land in an arroyo south of Triunfo Canyon Road, east of the Ventura County line, known as Three Springs Canyon. However, American-Hawaiian retained the area's development and recreational rights.

In August 1971, Boyle Engineering Company's plans for a dam were approved, and a $4 million contract was placed with Zern-Fraser-Wier for its construction. After installing steel anchors in the bedrock, construction of the dam itself was started. The 160-foot-high and 2,000-foot-long structure required the movement of 1.6 million cubic yards of material and was completed in the spring of 1972.

Since rain runoff to the 159-acre reservoir is about balanced by normal evaporation, its storage capacity of ten thousand acre-feet of water is supplied primarily from the Metropolitan Water District System. The $9 million filtration plant that treats the reservoir water, is located near the top of the dam, and was also designed by Boyle Engineering Company. Rex Murphy and M. R. Wallace constructed it with the first filtration run in May 1990.

In 1994, the Water District and the Santa Monica Mountains Conservancy acquired all the areas around the reservoir and the property descending east down to Triunfo Canyon Road. The city then reclassified the property as "Open Space." Some legal problems developed as a result of that acquisition, but were eventually resolved by the courts.

Las Virgenes Municipal Water District reservoir.

The City Seal

In January of 1982, the new city announced a contest for design of a City Seal. The local Security Pacific Bank branch donated $75, $50, and $25 savings bonds as prizes for the first-, second-, and third-place winning entries. A Council committee evaluated all those received and with the concurrence of the entire Council the winners were announced in April 1983. Walter Carlson, a South Shore resident and toy company executive was declared the first-place winner.

His design featured an acorn as background on which were emblazoned a book (for education, religion, and culture), a sailboat (representing Westlake Lake, sailing and water sports), and a horse (for the community's carefree and outdoor life).

That winning design was then presented to a graphics design company for review and final configuration. In view of the intended use as a logo and seal, the original design was then somewhat modified in that process. The acorn background was deleted, but the book, the sailboat, and the horse remained on the seal as it is used today.

174

City Seal with its designer Walter Carlson.

With very few exceptions, the city has enjoyed a surplus each year of its existence (Appendix B). Only the three fiscal years '90-'91 through '92-'93 were not surplus years with total deficiencies of less than $654,000—which were then made up in the following two years due largely by cutbacks in expenditures by the City Council. Cautious budgeting by successive City Councils has resulted in an enviable financial position relative to the great majority of cities in California. While most solvent cities work with reserves in the range of 5 percent to 25 percent over their normal budgets, Westlake Village holds a reserve in the range of 175 percent, even after some unusual "up front" costs associated with the design and construction of the new City Hall and Library.

From its inception in 1981, the City of Westlake Village has never levied any operating, gross receipts, or other fees or taxes on local businesses. Those businesses do pay property taxes to Los Angeles County—as do all home-owners—the city receives a return of only 5.8 cents on each dollar from such levies (one of the lowest tax-sharing rates in the county!). However, the city is fortunate in having some excellent sources of revenue from sales taxes even though it receives back only 1 cent of the 8.25 cents levied by the state and county. The city's sales tax receipts have risen from $1 million in 1990 to $2 million in

CITY OF WESTLAKE VILLAGE

1982-83
ANNUAL BUDGET

JUNE 23, 1982

The city's first budget.

1999. Another valuable revenue source is the Transient Occupancy Tax received through the Westlake Village Inn, which has increased to over $450,000 in 1999–2000 from less than $88,000 ten years ago.

The city also receives a variety of "restricted" funds, some thirteen in all, which by state or federal law must be used only for specifically designated purposes. The largest of these is the state gasoline tax fund, which in recent years

The city's current budget.

CITY OF WESTLAKE VILLAGE TWO-YEAR BUDGET 2002-03 & 2003-04

has exceeded $160,000. These monies are restricted to engineering, maintenance, and construction of streets within the city. The smallest of these thirteen funds is designated as OCJP (Office of Criminal Justice Planning) at $5,000, which is used for special traffic policing at school sites.

Among the "one-time" fees the city receives are those from building licences and permits. When the economy is strong, construction work is active and the fees increase accordingly. The city's income from these sources in 1993 (not a good year economically) was $150,000 and rose to $1 million in 1999.

By the end of 2000, there were 2.9 million square feet of existing office, commercial and business park space in the city, with another 327,000 square feet under construction. Plans for another 700,000 square feet are being reviewed. Employment in the city is currently 11,000, and the residential population in the year 2000 census was 8,368.

In support of the city's debt of $6,400,000 in Certificates of Participation to partially fund the new City Hall and Library, Standard and Poor assigned a rating of AA-, the highest rating for a city of our size. They also reported that Westlake Village had a median household income of $70,000, 208 percent of the state average.

As a "contract city," Westlake Village purchases most municipal services from outside sources. The largest contract, almost 45 percent of the city's budget, is with the Los Angeles County Sheriff's Department for police services. The contract covers, not only police car patrol, but also includes detective services, helicopter surveillance, and special team activities as required. Other contract services are all legal work, park and streetscape maintenance, street repair and maintenance, general engineering and traffic engineering.

The contract approach to city operation allows Westlake Village to operate with a staff of only nine people, from the city manager to the two part-time employees—the public works inspector and the city treasurer and financial manager. (Appendix M)

BUSINESS AND INDUSTRY

The first commercial buildings in the new community were the Westlake Village Inn and the nearby Chevron station—both designed by William Randolph, A.I.A., and built by Gattman and Mitchell. In 1970, both buildings received the Los Angeles Beautiful Community Awards.

The Westlake Village Inn restaurant (now named Provence) was built in 1968 and the first seventy-five hotel rooms were built just east of the Inn in 1969. Room rates were $12 per night and deluxe suites were available at $25. In 1993, the first all-suites building was opened with ten master suites and twenty business suites. The final phase opened in November 1996 with thirty-three minisuites, two luxury suites, and an elegant sixteen-hundred-square-foot, two-story suite. Rose gardens, water features, and a vined trellis that connects the Inn with the restaurants enhance the appearance of the property.

Entrance to Westlake Village Inn. (Courtesy Lussier Photography)

A First Neighborhood resident, John Brown, supervised the construction of a large factory facility on the west side of Lindero Canyon Road just north of the freeway, and as it was being built, he hired the employees from his rented trailer office. When the plant was completed, Brown also managed the operation of the Burroughs Corporation—in the manufacture of drum memory storage devices. The operation was later acquired by Memorex Company, and eventually was closed down. Two other early operations were located on the north side of Agoura Road. The Wilkinson Company specialized in precious metals, and the furnace used for smelting the gold and silver had a stack that looked like a tower on a Spanish mission. Nearby was a specialty heater manufacturer, Raypak Company, that occupied the site until 1997, when with no further room to expand, the operation was shut down and moved to Oxnard. Other operations along Agoura Road include State Farm Insurance Company, whose 755 employees occupy an attractive Spanish-style 257,586-square-foot building. The first section of the structure was opened on December 8, 1969. An addition was made to the building in 1975 and another of two stories was added in 1981. Nearby, on Sterling Center Drive, is a variety of medium- to large-size businesses. Among them, The Right Start, a company

Industrial park north of freeway, circa 1970s. Burroughs Corporation is located on the left.

179

specializing in children's clothing and accessories, which sells through stores at that location and in many other areas. It is a major telemarketer with a large bank of telephones where clerks take orders from around the world twenty-four hours a day. Another Sterling Drive major company is the Chatsworth Products, Inc. an employee-owned manufacturer of rack systems for major computer-using businesses, with manufacturing plants in Chatsworth and Redding, California; New Bern, North Carolina; Georgetown, Texas; and Newcastle, Indiana.

Chatsworth Products, Inc. (Courtesy Lussier Photography)

Pinkerton Security
International
Headquarters. (Courtesy
Lussier Photography)

K-Swiss. (Courtesy
Lussier Photography)

Most of the city's commercial and industrial operations are located north of the 101 Freeway and south of Thousand Oaks Boulevard. The area east of Lindero Canyon Road and surrounding the Valley Oaks Memorial Park was designated as the Westlake North planned development area for retail and business park uses. The largest of the operations is Costco, a membership store whose approval by the City Council resulted in disharmony by a minority group, which tried to launch a recall action against two Council Members. It failed. Numerous other large retail and fast-food restaurants occupy the area north of Costco, with business park buildings to the east, one of which is occupied by Homestore.com, a real estate referral service company.

The Spectrum Business Park is located on the south side of Agoura Road, east of Lindero Canyon Road. In addition to the new City Hall and Library, it includes among others, the headquarters of Pinkerton Security, the international investigative and protection agency; K-Swiss, a maker of high-end sports footwear; and Dakota Smith, an eye-ware specialty manufacturer.

Other major employers include Argent Technologies, which provides EDA software, and Condor Pacific Industries on La Tienda Drive, a provider of navigation and stabilization systems. Also, Trompeter Electronics on La Baya Drive which manufactures connectors and cable assemblies, and MWS Wire Industries on Cedar Valley Drive specializes in producing wires of all sizes, coated and uncoated in materials from aluminum to gold.

Dole Food Company, Inc. World Headquarters is located on the former Burroughs Corporation property between Lindero Canyon Road and Via Rocas, south of Via Colinas. In May 1998, construction work started on the three-story building of 180,500 square feet with a fourth level of 99,737 square feet below ground to accommodate

Lot 79

When some years ago, the city allowed the developer, Prudential, to pave Lindero Canyon Road from Hedgewall north to the county line, it was agreed that the city would be paid $400,000 for acquisition and/or development of park land, when and if available. In 1999, the city started negotiations with the owners of the open space, 41-acre parcel designated as Lot 79. The property spanned Lindero Canyon Road, with about 8.5 acres on the east side and the balance—a sloping hillside —on the west. In 1999, the city obtained an appraisal of $135,000 on the property, which by law was the limit the city could offer.

The owners did not respond to that offer and obtained their own appraisal. After a series of negotiations, the parties agreed to a purchase price of $535,000. Subsequently, the city arranged to sell the eastern 8.5 acres to the Las Virgenes Unified School District for $132,000 ($15,530 per acre) to allow access to Lindero Canyon Road from a new school to be built in Agoura Hills.

The final "out of pocket cost" to the city for the thirty-two acres on the west side of Lindero Canyon Road thus became $12,400 per acre.

About four years earlier, in anticipation of obtaining the land, the city had a design concept prepared for use of the property as a full-scale active park. There was considerable objection to that plan from the residents adjacent to the property and the Westlake Canyon Oaks Homeowner Association. If and when a future park is developed on the site, the city intends to work closely with nearby residents on the design.

Lot 79. (Courtesy Lussier Photography)

Groundbreaking of the Dole Food Company World Headquarters. Chairman David Murdock is in the foreground.

parking for two hundred vehicles. The building features an atrium that brings natural light into the structure, a large formal entry area and extensive use of finished wood throughout. About three hundred employees of Dole Food Company, Dole Fresh Fruit Company, and Dole Packaged Foods are currently employed at the facility, which also houses a testing laboratory, research library, an auditorium, and other amenities.

The most recent commercial construction is the twin office buildings project by Opus West on the north side of Agoura Road at the former Raypak site. Each of the two-story buildings includes 66,400 square feet of space. Farmers Insurance Company recently purchased the building paralleling the freeway.

The completed Dole Food Company headquarters.

The culmination of years of effort, analysis, and review was celebrated with pride on Saturday, March 23, 2002, with the Grand Opening of the new Civic Center.

While the city had occupied rental offices for many years, the desire for a "home of our own" was always in the minds of some of our city officials and residents. With the near certainty that the cost of rental property would continue to increase over the years to come, the economics of ownership was again studied in depth in 1996. Again the study indicated that, in the long run, ownership of a City Hall would be economically advantageous.

THE NEW CITY HALL AND DANIEL K. LUDWIG LIBRARY

The next step undertaken in 1996 and 1997 was to evaluate and select a location for a new City Hall and Library. Extensive studies were undertaken, with considerations to location, price, availability, and overall impact on the community neighborhoods. The sites studied included the office building next to Berniece Bennett Park, the park itself,

The new Westlake Village Civic Center. (Courtesy Lussier Photography)

Our new Civic Center. (Courtesy Lussier Photography)

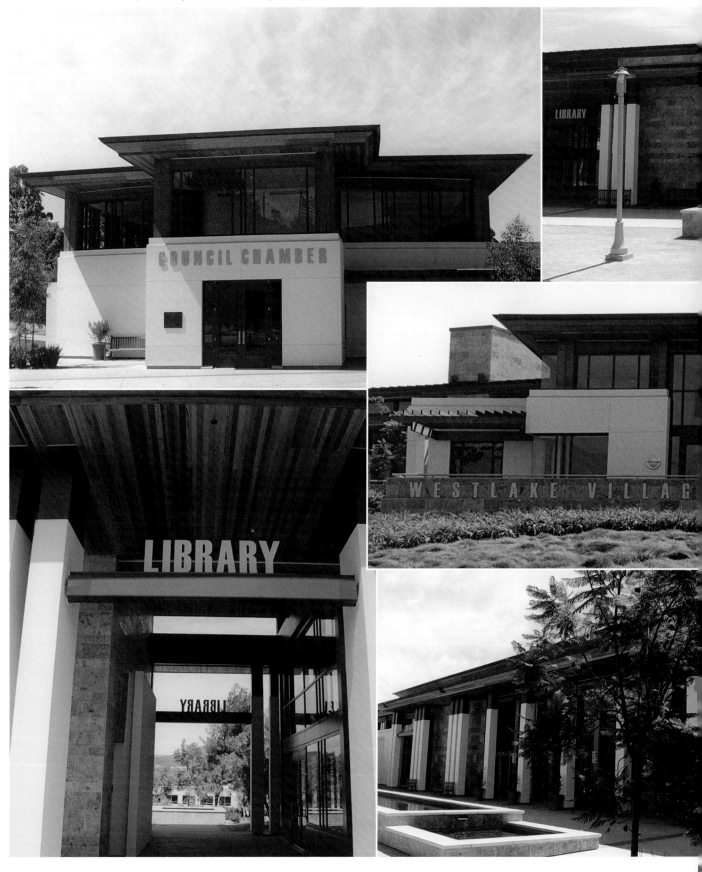

the Foxfield site next to the Fire Station, the former Security Pacific Bank building on Agoura Road opposite the County Line Shopping Center, and Lots 9 and 10 in the Spectrum Business Park. Results of those evaluations indicated the feasibility of two of those locations.

In April of 1998, the city mailed out postcards to every household soliciting opinions of the residents on which of the two sites would be most suitable—the Foxfield site or Lots 9 and 10 which were already owned by the city. On May 20, 1998, the City Council held a public hearing to review the survey results. With a high rate of response to the mailed survey, it was determined that the results were overwhelmingly in favor of building the new Civic Center on Lots 9 and 10.

The next step was to obtain a suitable design from a qualified architectural firm. After extensive efforts by city staff, a comprehensive Request For Proposal (RFP) was developed and circulated to over eighty companies. Eighteen firms had responded by the August 28, 1998 deadline. A screening of those proposals reduced the number of candidates to six architectural firms. A special interview committee comprised of Council members, staff, and consultants then interviewed the six semifinalists. The next actions undertaken were visits to the offices of the top three contenders to evaluate their facilities and to meet their staffs and management personnel. Those visits also included trips by Council and staff members to buildings designed by each of the companies and since some of

Community rooms under construction.

them were as far away as San Diego County, it made for some long days.

In order to assure the planned facility would cover the community's library needs, in November of 1998, the Council appointed a twenty-three-member Library Task Force to analyze and to make recommendations on library service options available to the city. The Council also signed a contract with Arroyo Associates, Inc., of Pasadena to perform a comprehensive feasibility study on the needs and options available. These studies were completed in about six months.

The Council then requested staff to initiate preliminary negotiations with the three finalists–CHCG Architects of Pasadena (later renamed CGA Architects), Fields and Devereaux Architects of Los

Angeles, and LPA, Inc., of Irvine. After much study, negotiations, and the overall evaluation processes, the Council selected CHCG Architects on February 10, 1999. The initial lump sum contract with CHCG totaled $432,000.

Civic Center architects Armando Gonzalez (left) and David Goodale.

Interior of new library.

The Council held the first in a series of workshop sessions on March 17, 1999, with the public and with CHCG Architects to develop ideas on the city's needs and concepts to guide the design process. On that same date, the Council approved a staff recommendation to establish rotating client teams of two Council members. The purpose was to meet periodically with staff members and CHCG on the several phases of the basic design.

Recognizing the need for professional oversight on a project of this complexity, the city issued a Request For Proposal to provide construction management services in early spring and seven proposals were received in response by the bid-closing date of May 21, 1999. In order to insure a readily workable layout for the Library, the city contracted on July 19, 1999, with Linda Demmers, a highly recommended library consultant, to work with CHCG Architects.

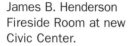

James B. Henderson Fireside Room at new Civic Center.

County Supervisor Zev Yaroslavsky, State Assemblywoman Fran Pavley, and Assistant Fire Chief Michael Dyer.

After reviewing the proposals for construction management services from a number of companies and after visits to several of their facilities, the Council approved a contract on July 27, 1999, with Swinerton Management and Consulting Services, Inc. The contract covered oversight of all design and construction details as well as establishment of a project budget. With that budget in hand, on September 22, 1999, the Council approved the schematic design of the City Hall and Library, at an overall "hard cost" budget for the project of $8.7 million. The Council approved detail design development for the project on December 8, 1999, and that effort was undertaken by the architect shortly thereafter.

Progress in the new year was somewhat delayed due to a January 2000 report in a geotechnical study that showed the necessity for soils remediation before any construction could commence. Grading of the site was also required to accommodate the design. On February 9, 2000, Swinerton Management reported to the Council on the results of soils test borings on both Lots 9 and 10 and on the need for stabilization. At that same meeting, the Council approved a change in the CHCG Architects' contract.

After studies of alternatives and in order to have the project proceed as rapidly as possible, the city opted to divide the project into two phases— the soils stabilization and grading work and the actual building construction. Accordingly, a contract was placed with Sharma General Engineering Contractors, Inc., on May 31, 2000, in the amount of $400,100. Grading on the site then started in June.

Prequalification studies by the city were undertaken during the summer of 2000. Requests for Proposal were then initiated for construction of the project with a bid deadline of August 31, 2000. After review of bids received from five contractors, the city selected Viola, Inc., of Oxnard and on September 5, 2000, negotiated a $7.6 million contract with a fourteen-month construction schedule.

On September 13, 2000, the city held a groundbreaking ceremony under a tent at the site. Many former Council members were in attendance, as well as other notables. After introductions and a brief overview of the projected construction by Mayor Iraj Broomand, the traditional "gold shovel" first turning of the soil was held. Many photographs were taken to mark the event and attendees enjoyed the refreshments provided.

The grading required in preparation for construction and the soils remediation work started on June 12, 2000, and was completed in about three months. The actual construction work started on October 3, 2000. The basic design of the structure is H-shaped, with City Hall facilities in the west leg, the Library in the east leg, and community rooms in the crossbar. The contractor had about three months of clear weather until work was slowed by rain. Construction started with concrete pad footings and floor slabs, after trenches were dug for all utilities with their piping and wiring stubbed out.

Erection of the steel beam moment frame followed, but some delays were experienced in steel

City of Westlake Village

CITY HALL/LIBRARY PROJECT
Groundbreaking Ceremony
September 13, 2000

The City Council welcomes you today, and expresses their appreciation for your attendance at this memorable event.

31200 OAK CREST DRIVE

Groundbreaking announcement.

190

deliveries to the site. Some other features of the unique design are towers with clerestory windows and copper roofs, extensive use of travertine marble both inside and out, interior cherry wood paneling and trim, and special wall fabrics. Redwood is used in many outside locations. Glass panels and doors are used extensively in the community rooms.

Water features are found in both the north (rear) and south (front) courts, and the latter is a large paved area suitable for many types of public events. While a few details remained to be completed on Grand Opening Day, March 23, 2002, the general opinions expressed were highly favorable—for the design, layout, and construction of the unique building.

City Council members, 2001–2002. Left to right: Councilwoman Susan McSweeney, Mayor Pro Tem Chris Mann, Mayor Betty DeSantis, and Councilmen Mark Rutherford and Robert Slavin. Ribbon cutting at grand opening of Civil Center, March 23, 2002.

The commemorative plaque at the Civic Center dedication, March 23, 2002.

Mayor Betty DeSantis greeting guests at Civic Center grand opening.

Dignitaries and attendees at Civic Center opening, March 23, 2002.

City Council members at commemorative plaque, March 23, 2002. Left to right: Chris Mann, Mayor Betty DeSantis, Mark Rutherford, Susan McSweeney, and Robert Slavin.

Trooping the colors at the Civic Center grand opening, March 23, 2002.

Docents ready to serve guests at grand opening. Docent Director Sally Bellerue is third from the left.

Scouts serving barbeque at the grand opening.

APPENDIXES

APPENDIX A

City of Westlake Village

Mayors

John H. McDonough	1981–1982
Berniece Bennett	1982–1983
Franklin Pelletier	1983–1984
Irwin Shane	1984–1985
Bonnie Klove	1985–1986
John H. McDonough	1986–1987
Berniece Bennett	1987–1988
Franklin Pelletier	1988–1989
Bonnie Klove	1989–1990
Kenneth E. Rufener	1990–1991
Berniece Bennett	1991–1992
James E. Emmons	1992–1993
Douglas R. Yarrow	1993–1994
Kenneth E. Rufener	1994–1995
James E. Emmons	1995–1996
Douglas R. Yarrow	1996–1997
Kris Carraway-Bowman	1997–1998
Betty DeSantis	1998–1999
Iraj Broomand	1999–2000
Mark Rutherford	2000–2001
Betty DeSantis	2001–2002

City Council Members

1981–1987
John H. McDonough
Berniece Bennett
Franklin Pelletier
Irwin Shane
Bonnie Klove

1987–1989
Berniece Bennett
Franklin Pelletier
Irwin Shane
Bonnie Klove
Kenneth E. Rufener

1989–1993
Berniece Bennett
Bonnie Klove
Kenneth E. Rufener
James E. Emmons
Douglas R. Yarrow

1993–1995
Berniece Bennett
Kenneth E. Rufener
James E. Emmons
Douglas R. Yarrow
Kris Carraway

1995–1997
James E. Emmons
Douglas R. Yarrow
Kris Carraway
Betty DeSantis
James B. Henderson

1997–1999
Kris Carraway-Bowman
Betty DeSantis
James B. Henderson
Iraj Broomand
Mark Rutherford

1999–2001
Kris Carraway-Bowman
Betty DeSantis
Iraj Broomand
Mark Rutherford
Chris Mann

2001–2003
Betty DeSantis
Susan McSweeney
Chris Mann
Mark Rutherford
Robert Slavin

General Fund Revenues and Expenses

Fiscal Year	Income	Expense	Excess (Deficiency)
1981-1982	$348,757	$128,866	$219,891
1982-1983	1,440,332	912,376	527,956
1983-1984	1,842,158	1,398,952	893,321
1985-1986	2,322,741	1,576,893	745,848
1986-1987	2,660,528	1,993,300	687,226
1987-1988	3,249,213	1,997,138	1,252,075
1988-1989	3,065,609	2,661,494	404,115
1989-1990	3,487,387	3,447,871	39,516
1990-1991	3,395,967	3,704,038	(308,071)
1991-1992	2,981,190	3,915,606	(34,416)
1992-1993	2,835,977	3,147,188	(311,211)
1993-1994	2,979,501	2,601,854	377,647
1994-1995	4,267,343	3,112,303	1,115,040
1995-1996	4,134,928	3,085,353	1,049,575
1996-1997	6,956,553	3,974,657	2,981,896
1997-1998	5,963,827	3,749,141	2,214,686
1998-1999	6,086,172	5,239,001	847,171
1999-2000	6,026,600	5,144,900	881,700
2000-2001	7,029,044	6,368,571	660,473

APPENDIX C

Citizen's Advisory Committees

Appointed May 5, 1982
Herbert Ashby
Pat Croner
Arnold Markowitz
Ray Brownfield
Lowell Corwin
Ann Lee Shane
Elsa Krebs
Harry Ailman
Leland Teets
George Galanis
Simon Perliter
Fred Kimball
Al Calcagno
John De Vore
Robert Herschman
Gil Reiner
Frank Sekula

Elizabeth Lawton
Nancy Dick
Jerry Doyle
Virginia Drasnin
Bill Springer
Rodney Hansen
Gary Woods
George Long
Kay Talwar
Jim Milner
Eleanor Winston
Walter Clifford

Appointed 1991
Bob Amenta
Sally Bellerue
Dick Bitting
Ray Brownfield
Jerry Carraway
Bill Carter
Jutta Clemmens
Carol Conte
Jim D. Johnson

Virginia Drasnin
Hal Feldman
Crosby Fentress
George Galanis
Steve Gavin
Walter Pahl
Ray Jassak
Elsa Krebs
Grant Magnuson
Arnold Markowitz
Dan Miller
Carlo Ohanian
Dick Philippsen
Ron Resner
Bob Riopelle
Bettina Salvodelli
Peggy Stivers
Dick Stone
Bob Thomas

APPENDIX D

**City of Westlake Village
Homeowner Associations**

First Neighborhood
Lakeshore
Oak Forest Mobile Home Estates
Parkwood Estates
Southshore
Summer Shore
Three Springs
Upper Terrace Townhomes
Watergate
Westlake Canyon Oaks
Westlake Colony
Westlake Cove
Westlake Island
Westlake Pointe
Westlake Renaissance
Westlake Terrace
Westlake Trails
WestPark Condominiums

APPENDIX E

Disaster Response Team Officers—2001
Jeff Friedman, Director
Larry Svoboda, Assistant Director
Sandra Kane, Secretary
Charly Kaspar, Treasurer
Bob Morrison, Member-at-Large
Deborah J. Gustafson, Member-at-Large

DRT Constitution Formulation Members—1995
Harold Feldman
Robert Morrison
Crosby G. Fentress
Joanne Robinson
Kris Carraway
Robert Beaudine
William F. Bogart
Toni Robinson Bogart
Sandra G. Kane
Deborah J. Gustafson
Martin A. Cohn

APPENDIX F

Meals on Wheels

Officers—1983
Janet Hollinger, President
(Chief Dietician, Westlake Community Hospital)
Kris Carraway, Vice President
Aelene McDonald, Vice President
Madeline Munroe, Vice President
Nora Sahagian, Vice President

Directors—1983
Bonnie Klove, Chairman
Bernice Schneider, Coordinator
Mary Duffy
Nan Lister
Gloria Caplan
Marsha Blackman
Betty Harmon
Jean Lee (Fundraising Chairman)

APPENDIX G

Westlake Village Preparedness Committee Appointments

January 11, 1984
For Public Emergency Services:
Mayor Pelletier
Sigi Ulbrich
Roz and Jeff Friedman
Charles Murray
John Stilo

For Utility Services:
Councilman McDonough
George Long
Jack Schweizer
Elsa Krebs
Howard Draper

For Facilities and Services:
Councilman Shane
Edward Cleary
Robert Allen
Sidney Drasnin
Edward Bidwell

For Life and Health Services:
Councilwoman Klove
Archie Latto
Frank Gillingham
Kenneth Rufener
Georgene Tack

For Transportation and Communication:
Councilwoman Bennett
Robert Weddle
Rod LeGate
Hal Carlson
Jim Parkinson

March 17, 1984
Harold Feldman
Brad Ormsby
Michael Berry
Anne LeGate
Sybil Nisenholz
David Melton

Sally Bellerue
Linda Metzger
Crosby Fentress
James Henderson

APPENDIX H

Revenue Sharing Allocation Committees

1984–1987
Eileen Clifford
Fred Onken
Gayle Reiner
Bettina Savoldelli
Donald Zimring

1987–1988
Michael Adams
Eileen Clifford
Bettina Savoldelli
Dolores Simon
Sigi Ulbrich

Community Service Funds Allocation Committees

1989–1990
William Bailey
Lillian Budell
Eileen Clifford
Bettina Savoldelli
Sigi Ulbrich

1990–1991
Kathy Anderson
Lillian Budell
Lynne Cavalier
Betty Robinson
Peggy Stivers

1991–1992
Rose Calhoun
Lynne Cavalier
Diana Malmquist
Peggy Stivers
Vivian Worth

1992–1993
Rose Calhoun
Lynne Cavalier
Diana Malmquist
Peggy Stivers
Vivian Worth

1993–1994
(No funds allocated)

1994–1995
(No funds allocated)

1995–1996
Berniece Bennett
Lynne Cavalier
Hal Feldman
Crosby Fentress
Diana Malmquist
Diana Skocypec
Richard Werner

1996–1997
Berniece Bennett
Lynne Cavalier
Hal Feldman
Crosby Fentress
Diana Malmquist
Diana Skocypec
Richard Werner

1997–1998
Sally Bellerue
Lynne Cavalier
Pamela Kelty
Phillipa Klessig
Tony Tramonto

1998–1999
Sally Bellerue
Lynne Cavalier
Pamela Kelty
Phillipa Klessig
Tony Tramonto

1999–2000
Douglas Smith
Tony Tramonto
Pamela Kelty
Fran Targon
Carol Kirschbaum

2000–2001
Sally Bellerue
Mel Flack
Pamela Kelty
Fran Targon
Carol Kirschbaum

APPENDIX H-1

Fund Allocations
1989

Action for Seniors	$3,000
American Youth Soccer Organization	1,000
Child Abuse and Neglect	2,000
Conejo Free Clinic	760
Hospice of the Conejo	3,000
Conejo Symphony	400
Senior Concerns	2,000
Conejo Youth Employment Services	1,000
Friends of the Library	3,000
Goebel Senior Center	1,000
Interface	2,500
Livingston Memorial Visiting Nurses	2,500
L. A. County Animal Control	1,000
L. A. County Sheriff	4,000
Open Door Counseling	1,500
White Oak Parent-Faculty Council	2,000
S.E. Ventura County YMCA	2,000
Sunday Afternoon Musicale	724
Villa Esperanza	1,000
Village Voices	700
	$35,074

Appendix I

Gann Limit Committee 1987

Member	Appointed By
Jim D. Johnson and James B. Henderson	Berniece Bennett
Steve Hessick and George Long	John McDonough
Tony Plaia and Donald Ronk	Franklin Pelletier
Robert Brune and William Wolff	Irwin Shane
Barbara Fentress and Kenneth Rufener	Bonnie Klove

Appendix J

1989 Housing Element Update Citizen's Advisory Committee

Col. James Hayes
Michael Sorrentino
Wlliam Springer
Sally Bellerue
John Moyen
Thomas Paltenghe
James Milner
Kris Carraway
Sybil Nisenholz
Juan Hernandes
James McGee

Appendix K

City Hall and Library Grand Opening Committee 2001–2002

Diana Malmquist–Chairman
Sally Bellerue–Docents
Dee Morrow–Event Food
Bill Chiaro–Donations
Mel Flack–Entertainment
Jeff Friedman–Public Safety
Berniece Bennett–VIPs
Joyce Prouty–City History
Pat McDonough–Volunteer Food
Terry Richardson–Business
Cheryl Tabbi–Entertainment
Marie Scherb-Clift–Library
Jim Henderson–History Book
and Audrey Brown

Appendix L

City of Westlake Village Volunteers in Policing—2002

Robert Benton
Michael Berry
William Calhoun
Barbara Fentress
Crosby Fentress
Diane Fentress
Brian Ladin
Fred Rosenberg
Vicki Terry
John Wolf
Robert De Santis, Program Deputy

Appendix M

City Staff—2002

Raymond B. Taylor–City Manager
Audrey Brown–Assistant City Manager
Robert Theobald–Planning Director
Peter Pirnejad–Associate Planner
Beth Schott–Deputy City Clerk
Linda Reed–Administrative Secretary
  and Accounting Manager
Shannon Ray–Administrative Secretary
  and Receptionist
* Robert Biery–City Treasurer
  and Financial Manager
* Robert McLaughlin–Public Works Inspector

* *Part-Time*

CONTRIBUTORS

Airey, Clint
Ashby, Herbert L., Justice
Austin, Victor
Bennett, Berniece
Bos, Robert C., Rev.
Bowman, Joseph
Brimhall, Grant
Brownfield, Ray C.
Carraway-Bowman, Kris
Commans, Amy
Emmons, James E.
Fish, Jack
Garretson, Roger
Greenbaum, Alan, Rabbi
Gold, Mary Lou

Goodrow, Donald
Hall, John
Hansen, Rodney and Margaret
Howse, Fred
Hus, Richard
Huse, Russell
Jassak, Ray
Johnson, Jim D.
Lawson, Robert B., Pastor
Marrewa, Marie
McDonough, John H.
Miller, Patricia Russell
Morrison, Robert
Nakano, Joanne
Notter, John L.
Poett, Harold
Prouty, Joyce and Ray
Rufener, Doris
Sprankling, Miriam
Taylor, Raymond B.
Tramonto, Tony
Zimring, Donald, Ph.D.

202

BIBLIOGRAPHY

Conejo Valley Historical Society Quarterly. Vol. 21, No. 3, 1976.

Development Plan for Albertson Ranch. Bechtel Corporation, 1965.

Gidney, C. M., Benjamin Brooks, and Edwin M. Sheridan. *History of Santa Barbara, San Luis Obispo and Ventura Counties.* Lewis Publishing Company, 1917.

Miller, Patricia Russell. *Tales of Triunfo.* 1985.

Russell, J. H. *Cattle on the Conejo.* Thomas Litho and Printing Company, 1959.

_____. *Heads and Tails.* Thomas Litho and Printing Company, 1962.

Shields, Jerry. *The Invisible Billionaire—Daniel Ludwig.* Houghton-Mifflin Coompany 1983.

203

204

James B. Henderson

James Beattie Henderson was born April 17, 1915, in Maplewood, New Jersey. His parents, James Bain Henderson and Ann Beattie Henderson, were Scottish immigrants. He married Lucille M. Riker on November 22, 1942. They have one daughter: Jill Henderson; two grandchildren: Eugene Furr and Heather House; three great-grandsons: Declan, Mason, and Colin Furr; and one great-grandaughter, Savanna House.

James attended local New Jersey schools and Newark College of Engineering, majoring in Civil Engineering. In 1936 he became employed as a draftsman with a Naval engineering company on design of Navy destroyers and cruisers. After engineering assignments with several companies, he worked in promotion and marketing. He joined Purolator Inc. in 1950 as Market Development Manager. He transferred in 1963 to become National Sales Manager, Aerospace Products, for PTI Inc. in Newbury Park, California. James was appointed Marketing Director in 1965. He moved to Westlake Village on February 5, 1968. He was assigned as PTI's Director of Engineering in 1980. Henderson retired in May 1983. He was elected to Westlake Village City Council in 1996.